CELEBRATING THE S

Celebrating the Small Church

MARTIN ROBINSON
AND
DAN YARNELL

MONARCH
Tunbridge Wells

First published 1993

Unless otherwise indicated, biblical quotations
are from the New International Version

ISBN 1 85424 232 6

British Library Cataloguing-in-Publication Data.
A catalogue record for this book is available
from the British Library.

Co-published with:

The Bible Society
Bible Society's vision is to equip the people of God with the resources
to make the Bible accessible and relevant to today's world.
Bible Society can be contacted at Stonehill Green, Westlea,
Swindon SN5 7DG.

The Church Pastoral Aid Society,
Athena Drive, Tachbrook Park, Warwick CV34 6NG. CPAS is a mission
agency which exists to strengthen churches to evangelise, teach and
pastor people of all ages. It seeks through people and resources to
stimulate evangelism, equip and train leaders, advise about ministry
and make grants for mission and training.

The British Church Growth Association.
The BCGA acknowledges the financial assistance received from the Drummond
Trust, 3 Pitt Terrace, Stirling, in the co-publication of this book.
For details please see end of book.

Produced by Bookprint Creative Services
P.O. Box 827, BN23 6NX, England for
MONARCH PUBLICATIONS
P.O. Box 163, Tunbridge Wells, Kent TN3 0NP
Printed in Great Britain

CONTENTS

INTRODUCTION

The small church is a survivor. The history of the Christian church bears witness to this single stark reality. But in the context of church life, small rarely means good. How then can we celebrate the small church? If what follows in this book conveys nothing else, it should communicate that the small church is not defined by numbers alone. In the words of Lyle Schaller, 'the small church is different' and needs to be approached as a unique institution, not as a scaled down version of a normal sized church.

The use of numbers, whether membership statistics or balance sheet figures, leads to a profoundly disturbing view of the small church. One analyst who looked at the American Episcopal church from this perspective concluded that, '43% of the clergy are serving 18% of the people in 62% of the parishes in a situation which is programmed for failure'. There is not much to celebrate in such a conclusion! But there are other more creative ways in which to view the life of the small church.

The authors have to confess a certain weakness for books on evangelism, church growth, and strategies for mission. Such titles occupy considerable space on our bookshelves. However, as we devour more and more volumes, we are aware that many if not all of these books presuppose, (whether consciously or not), a certain audience. These seem to be books written for and about churches which if not already large are certainly on the way to becoming large. The strategies that are suggested often require a level of resource, both in terms of money and people, that only a larger church could command. The church situations which are described would certainly seem to have something to celebrate–that is why they have been selected.

Perhaps more worryingly, we are told that in general, the leaders of small churches don't often read what we might broadly call resource books. We have no way of knowing if that statement is true but since most of the books we have described seem to be written for and about larger churches, it would not be surprising if it was an accurate assessment. Why then write about the small church? Is there really cause for a celebration of the small church?

At its most direct, this book on the small church came about because someone suggested that such a book was needed and after some thought the authors agreed. At a more fundamental level, we both owe a great debt to the small church because of a personal involvement with it that jointly amounts to a good number of decades. We have had to wrestle at a practical experiential level with the unique characteristics of the small church and in the process have come to love it with all of its blessings and frustrations.

In researching this book, both authors have been surprised and hampered to a degree by the relative absence of existing work on the subject. Certainly, in a British context, there are those who are working with the problems of the rural church and the inner city church. These churches often happen to be small, but that is not the same thing as writing about the characteristics of the small church as a unique phenomenon. Not all inner city churches and rural churches are small and the small church is found in other contexts besides these two.

We did find material written in the United States. Not the least of these is the work of Lyle Schaller, Anthony Pappas and Carl S Dudley. Anthony Pappas has established a network for small churches in North America which has its own news-letter, *The Five Stones*. However, although some of the charac-teristics of the small church in North America are similar to those in Britain, the context, problems and history of these churches is sufficiently different that not all of their insights are directly applicable to this side of the Atlantic. This is particularly the case because the definition of the small church used by these authors is generally that of the church of 200 or less. It is rather unlikely that a church of 150 to 200 would be considered small in Britain.

The lack of British research on the small church leads directly to two issues. First, it is important to regard this book more as an initial contribution than as a compilation of the fruits of research that already exists. It is very far from being the last word on the subject! The hope of both the authors is that this book will act as a stimulus for others to engage in further work on this subject.

Secondly, it raises the question of whether there needs to be a network for small churches in Great Britain. Such a network might further resource the small church by enabling churches to share their insights and by identifying the areas which require further work. To this end, we invite those who read this book to indicate their possible interest in a small church network by writing to:

Celebrating the Small Church
216 Maryvale Road
Bournville
Birmingham
B30 1PJ

The Structure of the Book

This book has been arranged in three parts. Part One attempts to describe the small church. Part Two concentrates on the particular problems of the small church, while Part Three offers some strategies that the leaders and members of small churches can attempt to implement.

In writing the book we have attempted to utilise the strengths of each of the authors, which relate to the perspectives each brings to this task. Martin Robinson works for the British and Foreign Bible Society as its Director for Mission and Theology. Before taking up this post he worked for the same organisation as a Church Growth Consultant. Dan Yarnell has recently celebrated ten years of pastoral ministry with a small church.

For this reason, Martin Robinson has written most of the chapters in Part One and all of the chapters in Part Three. Dan Yarnell has written most of the material contained in Part Two. Parts One and Three deal almost entirely with broader issues and strategies whereas Part Two centres more on what it feels like to be the leader of a small church with all of the practical problems involved. Inevitably, the individual styles of the two authors give a rather different feel to the chapters that each has written and there has been no attempt to produce a uniform style. The personal experiences and life stories of each author are reflected in the material that each has written and so, in the Contents page, the names of both authors are attached to the chapters that they have written.

The Church Means Mission

One other prejudice needs to be confessed. For both authors, mission is very high on their list of priorities. It has become rather commonplace to speak of Britain and Europe as mission fields, yet there is very little evidence that the church in our continent has changed its structures to take account of the surrounding mission field.

Some of the larger city based churches have taken the challenge of mission seriously. Their access to significant resources of people and money makes such churches particularly strategic in terms of mission, but it is unlikely that the activity of a few larger churches, no matter how creative they might be, will be enough to meet the missionary challenge of our age. It is essential that churches of every size are mobilised for mission. Paul Simmonds of the Church Pastoral Aid Society comments, '. . . if the church in Britain is to stop declining, it is the small churches which hold the key.'

In the wild savannah of Africa, there exist species of animals which are able to feed on every part of the foliage of the trees that grow there. The giraffes feed on the very tops of trees which are inaccessible to other animals. There is even a type of roebuck whose long neck and ability to stand on its hind legs gives it access to those parts of the tree that no other animal can reach.

In the ecology of mission, it will not be enough for only one type of church to be mobilised for mission. It will require the efforts of many churches of all types to make the kind of missionary inroads that our continent requires. It is our hope that *Celebrating the Small Church* will play a part in encouraging the small church to take its unique place in the ecology of the mission field.

Martin Robinson and Dan Yarnell

PART 1
Describing the Small Church

CHAPTER ONE

THE JOURNEY OF FAITH

As with most communities in South Africa, blacks and whites live and worship in separate communities in the town that I was visiting. That evening I was to speak to a large white congregation in Petermaritzberg. In the afternoon I went to speak to the local black congregation of the same denomination, which was very local and quite small. It was a form of worship that I was not used to. During my sermon the interpreter not only interpreted my words, he also interpreted my actions! At the end of the service the whole congregation gathered in two circles, one male and one female. The circles danced in opposite directions and each circle weaved in and out of the other so that we were able to greet and shake the hand of all those in the other circle. My dominant memory of that occasion was the huge smiles on each face and an overwhelming sense of welcome.

On another occasion, Easter Sunday, in a chapel in Britain, the clock chimed eleven o'clock and the worship began immediately, but neither myself or my wife could understand what was being said. The service in this small rural chapel was entirely in the Welsh language. Yet as the hymns were sung, the sermon preached and communion shared, a deeper language was being spoken. We were part of this family. Though the words were unknown to us the presence of God was very familiar, the warmth of the fellowship between the saints and the sense of being upheld by our participation in this event made us aware of saints before and saints beyond.

It was a Sunday night in Paris. My wife and I were the guests of a Tamil speaking church which met for worship in a side street close to the red light district in that city. The church building was rented from a French speaking congregation who themselves only rented what was in effect the ground floor of an apartment. The room was tightly packed with more than one hundred Tamil people. On a normal occasion we would describe this as a small church because they did not usually have so many present, but this was a special occasion and many had come from quite a distance. The majority of those who were present were refugees from Sri Lanka. A few were Tamils from India. Some had come from nominal Christian backgrounds and had found a personal faith for the first time in Paris. A good number were converted Hindus and a few were converted Muslims. Still others had not made a commitment at all. When in Sri Lanka, some of those present had lived in villages and had either been farmers or fishermen. Many had been trained as teachers or civil servants. One or two had been Tamil Tigers. As a social group they had little in common beyond their Tamil tongue and their refugee status, but as a worshipping group something very important was taking place.

These three small congregations could hardly be more diverse and yet despite the differences of language, worship style, tradition and even doctrine, all three congregations were inspired by a common vision and a shared encounter of the risen Christ. That shared encounter revealed to them a common destination, one that each of these three congregations would have been able to describe to the other two and agree that it was the same destination. But the precise details of the journey towards that destination were different in each case. All three agreed that they had not yet arrived. All three knew that they were involved in a journey of faith which necessarily meant that the details of the route were not always clear.

Not only did these three congregations share a common experience and a common conviction about their final goal, they also shared a common book, the Bible, which contains the record of many journeys of faith. The biblical account of the journey of the people of God is both inspirational and formative for his continuing people, the church, wherever it may be found.

God Calls a People

Genesis Chapters 12–22

It was always God's intention to call into being a people to whom He would reveal himself, and who would in turn bear testimony to the character of God. That call did not begin by selecting a people that already existed. Instead God called one man, Abram, who would be the father of a new nation.

God's call began with the explicit command to begin with a journey. Abram was to leave behind all that was familiar and to go to a new land. Interestingly the same call was given to Abram's father but he only went part of the way. Although the Bible does not make it entirely clear as to why Abram's father did not act on that revelation, the call was given afresh to Abram and he did respond. The Bible describes Abram on a number of occasions as a 'friend of God'. That relationship of friendship is ascribed to Abram's willingness to act in faith. His action and his faith are seen as inseparable parts of his response to God. His faith and his deeds are not seen in isolation. Both are important and both are given expression in the journey that Abram undertook.

Although the destination of his journey was clear and its purpose equally certain, the journey itself and the means by which God's purpose would be accomplished was nowhere near so obvious. Abram arrived at his destination, Canaan, but was soon on the move again. Before he had time to settle in Canaan a problem arose, in this case a famine, which meant that he had to leave Canaan in order to find sustenance in Egypt. In Scripture, Egypt is often used as a symbol for the temptation of God's people to seek the things of this world in preference to the destination that God intended for them.[1] Had Abram misheard God or was this merely a necessary detour on the journey that God had in mind? It is clear, not only in Abram's case, but later in the history of God's people, that the journey intended by God is not always ended so easily. The journey is long and hazardous even when the destination seems to be so near at hand.

Had God found in Abram a servant who was perfect in all respects? The Biblical account quickly reveals the shortcomings in Abram's life. His actions or reactions in facing the dangers of Egypt demonstrated a tendency to value self preservation over right action. His fears persuaded him to present his wife Sarai as his sister with almost disastrous consequences. The complex journey that God called him to undertake was important, not just because of the ultimate destination, but also because of what that journey was to teach him about the need to obey God and to exercise faith in Him.

The covenant that God made with Abram was repeated and renewed at a number of significant points in Abram's journey of faith. The most important renewal included an extension of God's promises. He was to have a son by Sarai. This step of the covenant was so significant that both Abram and Sarai had their names changed by God to the more familiar Abraham and Sarah. But even this significant foundational stage in Abraham's relationship with God did not mean an end to his travelling. Abraham continued to be a nomad both in the physical and the spiritual sense. The complex account of Abraham's journey of faith reached a critical and dramatic climax in the demand of God for Abraham to sacrifice his only son Isaac. Abraham's willingness to obey God, even in this harrowing matter, and God's deliverance of Isaac not only speaks of Abraham's journey of faith, but provides a rich testimony to the character of God's mercy upon which the children of Israel could draw during their own walk of faith.

God Delivers His People

Exodus Chapters 10–20 and Joshua Chapters 1–8

For the people of Israel, only their father Abraham was more important than Moses, the agent of God's deliverance. The theme of freedom and more crucially of the promised land, were seen in the light of the covenant promises made to Abraham. But once again, the journey had a significance of its own. It was not simply the means by which the people of Israel were to arrive at the promised land: the journey was valuable in its own right. It was for this reason that a journey which should have taken no more than a month actually took forty years.

The journey was the means by which the people of Israel were to be prepared by God for their entry to the promised land. They had much to learn about God, about their own lack of faith and about the intention that God had for them as a people. Such lessons were not always welcomed. A recurrent reaction was the emergence of bitter complaints. Why had they come at all? Difficult as life had been in Egypt, wasn't it preferable to their experiences in the desert? And when, finally, they came to the point where the Promised Land was before them, there was great fear. Wouldn't it be better just to stay where they were rather than enter the Promised Land with all the attendant risks and uncertainties?

The reactions of the children of Israel to their journey were understandable but they were also unrealistic. What would have happened if Moses had agreed to act on their complaints and returned to Egypt? Even if he had agreed that to go on was too difficult, there was no welcome waiting for them in Egypt. There really was no alternative but to press on with the journey.

The account in Exodus demonstrates that God always met the need of the people of Israel, but their constant desire to return, or at least to refuse to go on, would have brought any leader to the point of despair. However bad it has been in reality, the past tends to look much more comfortable than the unknown journey ahead. Yet it is to that unknown journey that the people of God are called. God does give guidance, and also sustenance, but the whole picture is not revealed ahead of time. The destination is clear but the precise details of the route, the timing and the events along the way are unknown. We only know that God has promised to be with us on the journey. The wilderness experience taught the people of Israel that God was with them and ahead of them. They needed to follow closely or there was a danger that they would be left behind.

A Missionary Journey

Jonah Chapters 1–4

The Old Testament makes it clear that God's promise to lead the people of Israel to a land that they would be able to call their own was dramatically fulfilled, but their arrival in the promised land did not complete their journey of faith. They still needed to be aware of the purpose for which they were called. The prophets of God made it clear that Israel's call was to be 'a light to the nations'.[2] They were to be the means by which the surrounding nations of the earth could come to know the character, person and will of God.

It soon became clear that this was not a part of the journey that they were anxious to pursue. Even by the time of the Exile they were not at all sure that God could be found outside of the boundaries of Israel itself. They had not been active in encouraging others to come to Israel to encounter the living God. Indeed most of their activity had been directed towards keeping aliens out. The glory, greatness and splendour of the God of Israel was only to be known in the extent to which he blessed and protected the nation regardless of whether they deserved such blessing. They were certainly not ready to engage in missionary activity towards other nations.

The one exception to this situation was Jonah. He was called by God to become a missionary to Nineveh, a journey that would normally be undertaken by sea. His immediate response to this challenging call was to take the first ship in the opposite direction. Try as he might he could not escape God's call. After his famous encounter with storm and fish he completed the first stage of his journey. But his successful arrival on the mission field was not the same thing as engaging in mission. At first sight the likelihood of success was not great. Nineveh was notorious for its evil deeds. Most people do not take very kindly to being told that they are evil, especially when the messenger is a foreigner and he is warning them of impending doom as punishment for their deeds.

To his credit, despite his initial response, Jonah was amazingly faithful in completing the task for which his journey was intended. However, he did not expect the astonishing accept-ance of his message by the residents of Nineveh and this very success produced a crisis for him. The book of Jonah records that the missionary preacher had wanted God to execute the disaster that he had preached about. He was far from pleased that God had taken note of their repentance and did not punish them. The final verses of the book reveal that it was not just the residents of Nineveh that had to repent. Jonah himself had to change as a result of his missionary journey.[3]

Unexpected Encounters

Luke Chapter 24:13–35 and Acts Chapter 9:1–30

Jonah was not the only one to be changed by his experiences on a journey. Saul was on a very different kind of journey when he set out for Damascus. The events that took place on that road are so well known that they have become part of the culture and language of the western world. 'A Damascus road experience' is a phrase which is part of our language and would be understood by many who did not share Saul's experience of the risen Christ.

It was a surprising journey to say the least. He began his journey as Saul and ended it as Paul. It began as a journey to persecute those with faith in Jesus and ended with Saul pro-claiming faith in Jesus. From the perspective of those who were Christians it was an astonishing journey. The most effective opponent that they had was to become their greatest champion as a consequence of the events on that road. Saul began the journey with physical sight but spiritually blind, he ended it with physical blindness but spiritual sight. It was not so much a journey of faith as a journey on which faith was found.

Saul, or Paul as we almost always think of him now, has not been the only person in Christian history to have had a dramatic and life changing encounter with the risen Jesus. Such encounters have usually led to a significant change of direction in the lives of those who have experienced them. However, we can hardly argue that Paul's Damascus road experience is normative in terms of the way in which people become Christians.

Perhaps most Christians more easily identify with those disciples on another journey in the Middle East. Following the events of the crucifixion and the reports of the resurrection, two disciples set out to travel from Jerusalem to Emmaus which Luke reports as being a journey of some seven miles. We do not know exactly how long they were travelling on that road, but the implication is that it took them some time since when they arrived at their destination, it was towards the end of the day. They had been joined by a stranger who had shared their conversation concerning the reports of the appearances of Jesus. The Scripture records that they invited their new found friend to stay the night and to share the evening meal with them:

> When he was at the table with them, he took bread, gave thanks, broke it and began to give it to them. Then their eyes were opened and they recognised him; and he disappeared from their sight.[4]

The risen Lord had been with them during the whole of their journey but they had not recognised him. It was only in the context of something familiar that they came to see who had been travelling with them. In retrospect they could understand who had been with them and why they had felt as they did at the time, but while on the journey it had not been so clear. It was only later that they could say 'Were not our hearts burning within us while he talked with us on the road, and opened the Scriptures to us?'[5] Their faith was nourished as they reflected on their journey even though it had not been so obviously a journey of faith at the time.

The fact that they had not understood the identity of their travelling companion during the journey did not make it any less significant. The gradual disclosure of the presence of Christ with them as compared with Saul's more dramatic encounter did not mean that they were less spiritual. One could argue that given Saul's murderous intentions on his journey, the reverse was true! Neither Paul nor the disciples on the road to Emmaus had expected to receive spiritual enlightment when they began their respective journeys. The unexpected took place as they travelled.

A Costly Journey

Luke Chapters 22–23 and Matthew Chapter 28

The journey which Jesus took, the journey to Calvary, has become an image that helps to describe the Christian life. The injunction to take up one's cross and follow Jesus acts as a powerful reminder that the Christian journey of faith is one that involves hardship as well as a promise of blessing. It is noticeable in the Scriptures that the disciples had great difficulty understanding and accepting that Jesus was going to have to suffer. These were not words they wished to hear. The disciples were much more pleased by the evidence of responsiveness on the part of the people during Jesus' triumphal entry of Jerusalem. They were not nearly as happy with the events at Golgotha.

The disciples' failure to hear the words of warning that Jesus gave had serious consequences. They were ill-prepared to understand the events surrounding the cross when they came. It was only later, after the resurrection events, that the significance and meaning of the words of Jesus could be understood. Then and only then could they fully understand what it might mean to 'count the cost' before beginning a journey of faith. Failure to count the cost might also mean failure to finish the journey, and the disciples quickly began to learn that the journey was almost as important as the destination.

Certainly the relationship with Jesus was to be one that constantly looked toward new horizons and did not allow time for complacency. It is noticeable in the Emmaus Road encounter that the stranger that accompanied the disciples seemed to be intent on going on beyond Emmaus. In Matthew's account of the resurrection appearances of Jesus the women were told by an angel of the Lord that 'He is not here; he has risen, just as he said.' Not only was Jesus not in the tomb, but he was already challenging the disciples to begin on their journey. They were not to stay where they were, they were to go on to Galilee where the other brethren would also see him. Their journey of faith was to begin straight away. Jesus could have appeared to them where they were, but already he was asking them to launch out in faith, to journey in faith, believing that what had been revealed to the women by the angel would be true. Matthew also makes it clear that the results of that journey of faith were mixed. They did all go to Galilee. They did all see the risen Christ, but some doubted. The results of our pilgrimage of faith cannot be guaranteed.

That same passage of Scripture contains some other words which also seem to stamp something of a hallmark on the journey of faith that Jesus calls his disciples to begin. 'He has risen from the dead and is going ahead of you into Galilee. There you will see him.' There is a strong sense that he is with us on the journey, encouraging and sustaining us even though we do not always recognise him. He is also ahead of us, preparing the way and suggesting that we need to keep moving forward if we are to see him more fully.

It is because he is always 'going ahead of us' that the people of God can only be true to their call when they are a pilgrim people. Frustratingly, the horizon towards which we travel may never seem to come any closer, but that does not mean that the journey is not worthwhile. However far ahead the horizon might be the journey itself is purposeful and significant. The destination on the horizon ahead of us is both our inspiration and our guiding light. We need that guiding light in order to find our way on our journey of faith.

A Church on the Move

These are only a selection of the journeys described in the Bible. There are a number of other important stories that we have not mentioned. The accounts of Israel's exile and return, and Paul's missionary journeys, are just some of those that have been omitted. However, we have described enough journeys to illustrate the simple point that the theme of being 'on the way' is basic to the intention of God for his people.

One of the earliest descriptions of the Christian community is 'the people of the Way'. Such a title is ambiguous. It can refer to the fact that the followers of Jesus were attempting to live the way of life or teaching that he had given to them. It could also refer to the fact that they saw themselves as citizens of a heavenly Kingdom towards which they were travelling. They were citizens here on earth but they were also citizens on a journey.

Such a description points to a fundamental understanding of what it means to be authentically the people of God, the church of God. There is no single cultural understanding, form or expression of what it means to be the church. Size, or other expressions of apparent success, are not the measurement for a local expression of the church. The most critical way of under-standing the true nature of the church is to see it as a people who are on the way, who know where they are ultimately going but are equally sure that they have not yet arrived.

There is an important sense in which the church can only truly be the church as it engages in the journey of God's missionary call. The problem for the whole church, to borrow an image from the wild west, is that we would much rather be settlers than pioneers. As soon as we become settled we lose touch with our founding charter and so fall short of our true potential. Like Abraham, we may be less than perfect, but God looks more at our willingness to respond than at our imperfec-tions. The desire to settle in one place may even involve a desire to look back at past achievements. But just as it was impossible for the people of Israel to go back to Egypt, so too with the church, there is really only the possibility of moving forward. To refuse to continue to travel does not safeguard what we have already, indeed it actually places it in jeopardy. The church which abandons the journey is a church which gradually ceases to be the church of Christ and becomes instead a social club.

To obey God and participate in mission means that we will change as much as those to whom we minister. The call to change and to be obedient to what God is doing in mission may bring a mixed response. Just as Jonah was angry with God, so we too might be at least puzzled and uncertain at what God does in mission. But our task is to seek to continue to travel and in relationship with God, to explore his future intention for us.

Our participation in that journey may occasionally mean changes that come to us in blinding moments of revelation. We may only see what God has been doing by reflecting on the journey itself. What is certain is that there is both a cost and a joy that comes to us from our participation in the journey to which God has called us. The journey is not one that we undertake alone, for the God who calls us is intimately involved with us along the way. He does not passively wait for us at the point of our destination, but is our fellow traveller.

My personal experience of travelling with God has mostly been as a member of a small church. I was brought up in such a church; I have ministered in small churches; I have engaged in church planting with small groups of people and although the small church is not my only experience of church life, it has certainly constituted a significant proportion of my Christian experience. That experience has certainly felt like a journey, but I know from my own past that the picture of the Christian life as a journey is likely to receive a mixed reception from the members of the small church.

On one hand, those in small congregations are happy that size is not the true measurement of the church. They know that this is true, but often stay quiet because they do not always have the theological tools to express this truth. The theme of journey helps those in the small church to see their own expression of the faith as important and as truly part of the whole journey on which the worldwide church of Christ is engaged. On the other hand, the theme of journey is not always welcomed by those in the small church because there is often a strong sense that the idea of being on a journey is more than they can bear. It is almost as if those in small congregations are having an extended rest from this journey of faith. They have often embraced the settler mentality simply as a means of coping with the many demands that are placed on the limited resources of the small church.

Although it is certainly true that congregations of every size can succumb to the settler mentality, often the small church is more prone to such temptation than other parts of the church. It is difficult to say in every case whether the tendency of a church to become content with the life of a settler is a major reason why a congregation is small, or whether the settler tendency occurs as a reaction to the failure to see numerical growth. Whatever the precise cause, it is rare to find small churches which might not be described as much more strongly in the settler than the pioneer category.

We cannot emphasise enough, however, that God does not call every congregation to be large, as if size itself was a measurement of what it means to be the church. His fundamental call is only for us to join him on the journey of faith, whatever that might mean for each local community of believers. For those of us who have tended to become settlers rather than continued travellers, God's word for us is to rejoin the journey. That decision might at times mean some pain and anguish. There is no guarantee of a journey that is certain and trouble free. We can almost be sure that the reverse will be true. Nor does God ask us to wait until our congregation is perfect before we begin the journey. He can only form and shape his church once we are on the way.

Notes

1. This view of Egypt is seen most clearly in the prophetic warnings given to Israel which advise against making treaties with Egypt against the Assyrians. See especially Jeremiah Chapter 44.
2. The phrase 'light to the nations' is used a number of times in the Old Testament but perhaps the best know reference is found in Isaiah 49:6.
3. For a very helpful commentary on Jonah see Jacques Ellul, *The Judgement of Jonah*, (Eerdmans: Grand Rapids, 1971).
4. Luke 24: 30,31.
5. Luke 24: 32.

CHAPTER TWO

THE SMALL CHURCH ON THE FRONT LINE

My father had a habit of planting churches. He planted churches on the mission field in India and then returned to Britain to do the same in his own land. The first British church that he planted was in Scotland. He has since planted at least three more churches in England. The circumstances in which these churches were planted meant that they were all small. Most of them began in homes and grew slowly. Partly for that reason I have spent most of my life worshipping in small congregations. My father has spent even longer doing so. Not that it has ever worried him. He grew up in a small congregation in London, which worshipped in a 'tin tabernacle'. He (and I) have been part of a denomination which has consisted largely of small churches. Both of us have seen first hand that small churches can be good places to be. We know that great things can come from them.

But what exactly is a small church? Are we referring to the number of members, or to the number of people who attend worship? Or are we referring to numbers at all? Do we really mean the size of a church's vision or its quality of commitment? Inevitably the very word 'small' draws us back to the question of figures, however important other factors might be. So for the purposes of this book, we have somewhat arbitrarily chosen the definition of 50 adults attending a normal worship service as a small church.

Even though we have used numbers to define what we mean by a small church, numbers alone do not adequately describe a small church. Many of the later chapters of this book will paint in a variety of ways some of the qualities that are uniquely present in the small church. But there is one particular factor which needs to be described which lays down a critical marker for what it means to be a small church.

The American researcher Carl S Dudley has made some useful observations on the nature of the life of small churches. Writing in a paper called the *Unique Dynamics of the Small Church*, he notes that true small churches are *single cell organisations*. In other words, in such a church the members all expect to know each other personally. This does not mean that they have very intimate relationships with every other person in the church but it should be possible for them to know a good deal about every other person in the church. In Dudley's words:

> They can 'place' the other members by where they sit in worship, whom they are related to in the congregation, and what part they play in the social economy of the 'village' (rural or urban).[1]

They may not know the complete history of each person in the congregation, nor everything about what they like and dislike, but they would certainly expect to know something about such matters as how many children each person had and how they earned their living.[2] This description of the small church as a single cell organisation helps us not only to understand something important about what we mean by the term 'small church', it also helps us to recognise that there are some churches which might qualify in numerical terms as small but which are clearly a different kind of animal altogether. Let me describe two such other 'animals'.

The first is the church which is newly planted and has therefore started life as a small church but which is only temporarily small. Dudley describes a review of new church developments that took place in the 1960's. The method of church planting that was being reviewed was that of using an organising pastor to begin a number of cell groups which were only brought together to launch the church when sufficient people had been attracted. Some pastors were very able to integrate the various cell groups into one big happy family.

Other pastors had more difficulty in producing easy relationships between the various groups. Perhaps unexpectedly, it was the churches which 'jelled' the most quickly that stopped growing, whereas the churches which had experienced some degree of tension between the various groups went on to become larger churches.

How could this be? Put very simply, the cell groups which merged easily became a single cell organisation and so qualified very easily as a small church, whereas the churches that were less successful in producing a happy marriage of groups remained as multiple cell organisations and thus retained the basic building blocks for a larger church. This outcome illustrates very well both the strength and weakness of the small church. The small church is often a happy church, content with the intimacy of the single cell situation. The larger church may also be a contented church, but it is so because a variety of people can find a place within a more complex organisation.

The second 'animal' which might well qualify as a small church on a numerical basis but which does not meet the criterion of a single cell organisation is the larger church which is temporarily broken. Some churches which may have had a larger attendance for most of their existence occasionally experience a crisis of some kind which for a time severely reduces their attendance. Such a church will rarely be happy as a small church. It needs healing in order to become once more a larger church.

So by a small church we mean both a church which normally has 50 or less adults in their main worship service, and which is typically a single cell organisation in the sense that most people in the church feel part of a single family within the church.

The Small Church is Normal

Small churches generally do not make the headlines. Many Christians will have heard of the Full Gospel Church in Seoul, Korea, which is pastored by Yonggi Cho and reputed to be the largest church in the world with close to 750,000 members. Many will also have come to know something of Willow Creek Community Church, the second largest Protestant church in North America which seeks to 'build a church for the unchurched'. In Britain many Christians will know of a church such as All Souls, Langham Place, or Charlotte chapel in Edinburgh. More locally, Christians will be aware of some of the larger churches in their immediate town or city. They may well be able to say something of what such larger churches are like even though they have never attended. It is quite likely that they will know the name of the minister of such a church, especially if he or she has been there for some time. It is far less likely that a small church will ever be as well known. On a number of occasions when I have been seeking directions for a small church, some people in a community seem totally unaware that such a church even exists.

Not only are small churches not well known, as individual congregations they rarely influence the wider Christian world, establishing new trends and shaping the agenda of the wider church in evangelism, social action or worship. They do not make a great deal of impact on denominational policy. Their leaders rarely move directly from membership or ministry in a small local church to positions of influence within the denomination. Yet however much we might detail the lack of impact that small churches make beyond their immediate circle of influence, the small church is vitally important for the future of the whole church. To put it very simply, most, though not all, churches have been small at some point in their existence. There have always been and there almost certainly always will be small churches in our midst. The small church, therefore, matters and does so for four key reasons.

The small church represents the normative present experience for many millions around the world

There are at least four factors in relation to the small church in Britain which highlight the extent to which they are part of the normative experience of Christianity for a significant portion of the faithful. First, the sheer number of small churches is very high. According to the 1989 Marc Europe Census figures, some 36% of all churches in England have a weekly adult attendance of 50 or less. Other research suggests that the true figure may even be somewhat higher than this. In any case, even 36% of the 39,000 congregations in England represents just over 14,000 congregations.[3]

Secondly, their geographical location. Research conducted by the Bible Society in 1991 suggests that 75% of churches with 25 or less adults in worship on a Sunday are to be found in rural areas. 61% of churches with 50 or less adults in worship on a Sunday are found in rural areas. In other words, the smaller a church is, the more likely it is to be a rural church. Another way of looking at the statistics is to say that 62% of all congregations in rural areas have 50 adults or less in attendance on a Sunday.

Not surprisingly, when we look at the Marc Europe figures for whole areas of the country, we find that the more rural they are the higher the percentage of small churches are to be found in that area. So 57% of churches in Somerset, 69% in Lincolnshire, 63% in Shropshire, 53% in Cumbria, 60% in Norfolk. 64% in Cornwall and 53% in North Yorkshire are all small churches according to this numerical classification. In other words, there are large areas in our country where the normal experience of church life is that of the small church. These regional figures are given added potency when we realise that in virtually all of the examples given above the percentage of small churches among Anglicans, where rural rather than small town churches are more numerous, show even higher percentage figures. In Lincolnshire for example 76% of all Anglican churches fall into the category of small churches.

It is much more difficult to obtain figures for inner city or urban priority areas, but the statistics that are available demonstrate that these areas of our land represent an additional landscape where the predominant experience of church life is that of the small church. This tendency can be illustrated by reference to the difference between Inner London and Outer London. In Inner London, which includes some of the larger city churches such as All Souls and Holy Trinity Brompton, 33% of all Anglican churches are small churches, whereas for Outer London the equivalent statistic is 19%

Thirdly, denominational affiliation. There are very large differences between the denominations as to the percentage of small churches in their midst. The older, historic protestant denominations have far higher percentages of smaller churches than the newer Pentecostal and Charismatic house churches. For example, in 1989 51% of Methodist congregations were small compared to 19% of Pentecostal churches. The Roman Catholic Church has by far the least number of small churches when one uses the statistical guideline of attendance in worship —some 3%. Although it is certainly true that the newer denominations are growing much more quickly than the older denominations and that they are planting many more churches, we always have to remember that their growth takes place from a much smaller base. In other words, the spread of churches across Britain is such that it is far more likely that a community will have contact with a congregation that is part of the one of the historic denominations than they are to be located close to a Pentecostal or House church congregation.

Interestingly the percentage of small churches in the various denominations has remained largely constant among Methodists, Anglicans and the United Reformed Church over the last ten years, but among the Baptists, Pentecostals and House churches, the last ten years has seen a significant change. There are now far fewer smaller congregations among this latter group of churches, which seems to be an indicator of their more general growth patterns. For example, in 1979 43% of Baptist congregations were listed as small compared to only 28% in 1989. The Pentecostal figure of 19% in 1989 had fallen from 42% of congregations in 1979.

Fourthly, the length of time that the congregation has been established. In very general terms, the longer a congregation has been established the more likely it is to be a small church. To some extent this issue overlaps with the question of geography since there is a higher percentage of churches in rural and inner city areas which have been established for many years than would be the case in suburban areas. However, even within the suburban scene this same generalisation would appear to be true.

A very typical profile of the small church would therefore be a congregation which is from one of the historic Protestant denominations, is located in an inner city or rural area and which has been established for many years. That profile is sufficiently normative that most people in our land could picture such a church even if they have never attended one. We are not dealing with a rare and unusual breed! Such churches have touched and continue to touch the lives of many Christians throughout the land.

The location of small churches often represents the front line of mission

The very areas where Christian witness is at its weakest is where small churches are the most numerous. This is especially true of inner city and rural areas. It is all too tempting for Christians in larger suburban or city centre churches to see the smallness of churches in inner city and rural areas as an indication that such churches have failed in their mission. Small churches therefore represent a primary reason for the weakness of the Christian faith in areas of need. Seen from this perspective small churches are signs of failure rather than beacons of hope.

Such a conclusion needs to be tempered by two reminders. First, the churches in rural areas often achieve a percentage penetration of the population that surrounds them which larger suburban churches rarely if ever match and yet still remain small. I visited a family in one rural area which lived in a village of just 60 people and yet which managed to maintain its own parish church. The average attendance for many years had been six people, or 10% of the population. Recently attendance had at least doubled representing at least 20% of the population. More significantly, a midweek bible study, discussion and prayer group attracted close to 20 people, or one third of the population, while the Harvest Festival Supper was attended by 45 out of the 60 people in the village! Few suburban churches would ever attract such high percentages of their immediate population.

If the first reminder relates more strongly to the rural scene, the second reminder draws on the experience of churches in the inner city. They often witness to communities which have been significantly unchurched since the beginning of the industrial revolution. Commenting on the results of the census of 1851, one Christian leader noted:

> More especially in cities and large towns it is observable how absolutely insignificant a proportion of the congregation is composed of artisans. They fill, perhaps, in youth, our National, British, and Sunday Schools, and there receive the elements of a religious education, but no sooner do they mingle in the active world of labour than, subjected to the constant action of opposing influences, they soon become as utter strangers to religious ordinances as the people of a heathen country.[4]

This state of affairs arose before the flight of middle class Christians to the suburbs took place. The writer quoted above goes on to make the clear point that those who were becoming increasingly unchurched lived on the doorsteps of large and successful churches. The frontier of Christian mission in the inner cities has much more to do with the failure of large churches whose members (and sometimes whose buildings) abandoned the inner city many years ago, than with the failure of the small churches which are now present in these areas.

The presence of small churches both in the inner city and in rural areas is the only viable Christian witness that is available. For this reason it is important that the life and witness of small churches on the cutting edge of mission should be as effective as possible.

Small churches often have access to unique networks of people

The small church is a caring church. There is very little expectation in the small church that the care extended by its members is going to produce large scale growth. Rather, care is seen not in terms of potential evangelistic growth, but simply as something that the small church does because of the emphasis it places on people and relationships. The long term impact of such care often produces a situation where there are many in a given community who regard the small church as somehow the church that they are part of even if they do not attend any worship services.

Some years ago I encountered a small church which had been

strongly advised to close down because, from the perspective of the denomination that they were part of, the church was no longer viable. Not surprisingly the 18 members resisted this suggestion and were sufficiently spurred into action to engage in some door to door visitation in the community. Part of their activity involved a survey of what churches people in the community belonged to. They were surprised to discover that something like 100 people in the neighbourhood regarded their small church as the church that they belonged to even if they never actually attended it. The members of this church were puzzled by this situation. How was it that so many people considered that this was their church? The answer seemed to be that many of these people had experienced care of some kind from members of the church over a long period of time. In terms of the attitude of the community many small churches are larger than they imagine themselves to be.

It is important to understand that this long term investment of care often produces a situation where there is a network of people in the community who not only look sympathetically towards a small church that they don't attend, but these same people form a network that probably cannot be reached by any other group of Christians. Such networks often extend beyond those in the immediate community to whole families of people who either attended the Sunday School, or a youth activity as children, or whose own children, and in some cases grand-children, had a similar contact. Many of these families may no longer live in the immediate community but form a circle of contacts which can be activated under the right conditions.

Small churches are often rich bearers of valuable traditions

The Christian faith does not consist of one expression of the faith but is enriched by the variety of local expression. This variety is expressed in the small church in at least two ways. First of all, small churches have often adopted a particular expression of the faith in order to relate strongly to the soul of particular communities. They understand their surroundings and have adapted to meet particular local needs. Secondly, small churches are often faithful transmitters of a particular local heritage. Traditions are easily and naturally maintained in the small church.

Perhaps surprisingly it is often smaller churches that are the strongest supporters of denominational life and witness. The variety of small church life is bound together through such denominational allegiances. There may not be a well thought through theology of why things are done the way they are, but there will often be a strong commitment to maintaining particular distinctives, not in a sectarian manner, but simply as faithful witnesses to traditions that many have found to be valuable. It is almost as if small churches add something to the total genetic reserves of the faith which without their witness might be lost completely.

For these and quite possibly other reasons, small churches represent important ingredients in the total mission force which is the church in the modern world. The way in which the small church lives out its life will collectively be significant as the church strives to discover the role that God has for it in a rapidly changing world.

The Small Church is Under Pressure

We were in a small gathering of some dozen clergy drawn from various parts of the United Kingdom. The men who were present were all from very different sizes and types of church. All had a wide experience of church life and were aware of the kinds of issues that were occupying the attention of the church. One minister began to share something of his own situation. He had pioneered a church on a large council housing estate at least twenty years ago. They had had moments of triumph and had seen many precious conversions through the years. Some from their church had gone into ministry elsewhere and others had moved away to become faithful members of other churches. Few, if any, Christians had transferred from other churches to join them. At this particular time they were at a low ebb. The church had just passed through a leadership crisis and the man in question had returned after an absence of some years to take up the burden of leadership once again.

He reflected that his church had about 18 adults in regular attendance. In times past there had been more but they had always been a small church. He commented that the estate consisted of about 20,000 people and he described the sum total of Christian witness on the estate. There were three other churches and the combined membership of all the churches barely scraped 100 people. He knew from his experience that this was not a unique situation. Our brother's comment made us stop and keep silent for a time. He said, 'There are an awful lot of small churches out there which are hanging on by the tips of their fingers'. We all knew that he was right and that for all our varied experience none of us had any easy answers to offer.

Many small churches are under pressure at this time. Why? After all we have indicated that there have always been small churches and probably always will be. Why should so many feel as if they are only just hanging on?

In large measure this is caused by a number of key societal changes. First and foremost there is the factor of choice. It has always been possible to choose from a number of churches in the city, but there has been a growing trend for people to be increasingly mobile in many aspects of their life. People travel further to shop, to work, to socialise and to play than they ever did before. Even in rural areas mobility is an increasing factor which means that people do not have to think too hard before deciding to worship outside of their immediate community.

Along with this increased habit of mobility is a sense that people have greater expectations from their church concerning the standard of worship, fellowship and programme. If they feel that their local church is not providing what they want, then they are able and willing to travel in order to obtain what they are looking for. Consumerism has affected the market place of religion as much as many other market places. Clearly it is far more difficult for a small church to provide a first rate music group, choir, children's programme, youth activity and preaching standard.

Nor can small churches any longer depend on denominational loyalty to keep someone worshipping with them when there is a church which seems to meet their utilitarian needs far better, even though it is of a different denomination. All the evidence available suggests that denominational affiliation comes increasingly low on the list of priorities that those who are looking for a new church have on their shopping list.

Even the ingredient of family ties which used to be a strong point for small church life is growing increasingly rare as a recruiting agent. At one time one might expect to find three if not four generations of a single family in one church. Today such a phenomenon would be rare indeed. When teaching seminars I often ask those who are present how many are worshipping in the same church in which they grew up. It is unusual to find any who are. Why should this be so? The generally increased mobility of our population means that professional couples are very unlikely to remain in the same community in which they grew up. In addition, a far higher percentage of Christian young people attend higher education as compared with the population as a whole. This single factor almost always requires a move to be made and it is not often that a young person will return to their home church once they have been away to College or University.

In short, many of the same factors which have put the corner shop under pressure and caused supermarkets to become a dominant part of commercial life apply, albeit in a more complex manner, to small churches. Life is not easy for the leader of the small church. One senses that the leaders of many small churches are tired. At one time they might have expected the next generation to take over in the youth club or the Sunday School. Now they find that the next generation are worshipping in a larger church in another city and they are still doing the jobs that they have done for far too long.

Yet the fact that the small church is under pressure does not make it any less important. One senses that, unlike the corner shop, the small church is not going to go out of business. But what matters is not just that the small church stays in business, but that it is able to discover a *joie de vivre* in going about its task. The small church can and should be a happy place in which to be.

Notes

1. Carl S. Dudley, 'Unique Dynamics of the Small Church', *Special Papers and Research Reports*, The Alban Institute, Washington, p7.
2. For a more detailed description of the expectations of those in the small church see, Carl S Dudley, *Making the Small Church Effective*, (Abingdon: Nashville, 1978), p 35.
3. Unless specifically credited to research conducted by the Bible Society, the statistics in this section have been extracted from *Prospects for the Nineties*, (Marc Europe, 1991). This information was taken from the *1989 Church Census* conducted by Marc Europe. Following the closure of Marc Europe, much of the work undertaken by this organisation has been continued by the Christian Research Association.
4. James R Moore (Ed), *Religion in Victorian Britain*, Vol III Sources, (Manchester University Press: 1988), p 315.

CHAPTER THREE

THE MANY FACES OF THE SMALL CHURCH

The pressures which afflict the small church today are not unique to small churches, but they often impact small churches more acutely than churches which have access to a greater level of resource. The dominant fact of our time that influences all religious life is that of the reality of secularisation. The idea that life can be adequately explained and lived without any reference to God at all has become an unstated assumption in much of our public life. Yet despite such pressure, religious conviction has not just disappeared as it was once expected to do. Surveys on religious values consistently display a surprisingly high degree of religious belief. Something close to 70% of British people claim to believe in God and an even more surprising 64% claim to be affiliated to a denomination.[1]

Despite these relatively high levels of residual religious conviction, and the claim of 58% of the population to have confidence in churches, those who are active members of congregations know only too well the degree of reluctance that most people in every community have to the prospect of actually becoming part of a local church. The reality for the greater part of church life during most of the 20th century has been one of decline in the face of a changing society. This decline has not only ensured that many churches have become accustomed to being and remaining small, it also means that many small congregations have closed their doors.

A challenging aspect of the secular culture that surrounds us is the very pace with which change takes place. The English church historian Adrian Hastings, reflecting on the attempts of the church to adapt to modern life comments:

> A trouble with modern culture is the sheer speed with which it goes through things.[2]

Alvin Toffler, the writer of *Future Shock*, was the first popular writer to draw attention, not only to the rapidity of change, but the extent to which the pace of change continues to accelerate. He quotes the economist Kenneth Boulding:

> The world of today . . . is as different from the world in which I was born as that world was from Julius Ceasar's. I was born in the middle of human history to date, roughly. Almost as much has happened since I was born as happened before.[3]

The small church is often seen as a place which acts as a haven of peace, safe from change. One line of a traditional hymn which describes the church as a safe refuge ends one verse with the line, 'For nothing changes here.' In one sense this can be a positive virtue. Such matters as truth, honesty, integrity in relationships and many of the other aspects of Christian life should not change. But the cultural expression of Christian life and worship necessarily needs to change if the church is to remain in contact with the world to which it seeks to witness. The means by which the unchanging truths of the gospel are declared will inevitably need to be reconsidered if communication is to take place.

In the words of a recent pop song, 'constant change is here to stay'. But the kinds of change that impact the small church vary enormously, depending to a great extent on the geographical location of a particular congregation. The remainder of this chapter will concentrate on examining the very different challenges that face small churches as a consequence of different social settings.

The Small Rural Church

It is tempting for suburban and urban Christians to have a somewhat romantic view of the relationship between the church and its parish in the countryside. As David Holloway puts it:

It is often said that in rural areas more people go to church than in urban areas. This is because, it is argued, the church in Britain is more at home in rural areas—it had its roots in a rural, not urban, society.[4]

To some extent this romantic folk memory imagines that there was a time, a golden age before industrialisation, when most people lived in the countryside and attended church. There is little hard evidence for such a view. Commenting on this idea of a 'golden age' in English church life, Andrew Greeley writes:

> Instead, some scholars are beginning to question whether there was all that much devotion in western Europe even in the high middle ages. Finke and Stark 9 (1992) note that most medieval rural churches were far too small to provide room for all the people in their parishes, and cite evidence that in 1738 thirty Oxfordshire parishes reported only a combined average total of 911 communicants on the four great festivals of Christmas, Easter, Whitsun and Ascension.[5]

A footnote in the same article points out that in Yorkshire in 1743 only 20% of adults attended worship regularly. While it is true that the Victorian period saw generally higher levels of church attendance than in the 18th century, the concept of a rural church which acted as the centrepiece of popular devotion in pre-industrial English life is almost certainly a myth. Moreover, the dominant reality of English rural life for the greater part of the 20th century has been one of depopulation, with large numbers of people abandoning the countryside for life in the towns and cities of England. Understandably the movement of population away from rural areas undoubtedly weakened church life in the countryside.

Despite a gradual decline in population, however, it could be argued that little else in rural life changed and so it is still tempting to adopt a view of country life as offering a large degree of stability in the face of gradual change. That may once have been true, but has certainly not been the case more recently. The 'Faith in the Countryside' report produced by the Church of England comments:

Almost every aspect of rural life has altered significantly since the Second World War. There have been substantial shifts in the structure of the rural population, traumatic changes to the patterns of agricultural production, new problems associated with the emergence of a changed working base for the rural economy, and social transformations arising from the movement of growing numbers of professional people out of the cities into the rural areas. Not surprisingly, the consequence of such change has been increasing tensions in rural life.[6]

The same report points out that the countryside has not been immune from the more general changes in our culture:

For the growth of individualism is affecting and destroying community life in many rural areas. Some of the views of the person which we have outlined in this chapter, those of self-determination, privacy and isolation, have been carried into the rural areas and have made the village a very lonely place.[7]

Ironically, the very values that seemed so attractive to those who have moved into the countryside have been eroded by the sheer numbers of those who have made such a move. Perhaps without those same newcomers realising it, '. . . population movements have brought new people with different perceptions and ambitions into rural life.'[8] It soon becomes clear that these significant changes bring both opportunities and immense challenges to the small Christian congregations that seek to minister to people in rural areas.

One Anglican vicar who has spent most of his ministry in rural congregations told me that he generally found that he had to minister to four quite distinct groups of people. He described them as follows. First there were the original people who still either work on the land or have strong family connections with agriculture. Secondly there were those who had retired to live in the countryside. Thirdly there were those whom he called 'the lentil and beans brigade'. This group was diverse, mainly consisting of those who were looking for an alternative lifestyle and who had to a greater or lesser extent dropped out of mainstream secular life. The fourth group comprised those younger professional couples who were using the countryside as a dormitory area, because they still earned their living in cities or larger towns but commuted from a home in the country.

The essential point my friend was wanting to make about all four groups was that their expectations of the church were not only different but were in direct conflict with each other. In his experience those who had retired to the countryside often wanted nothing in the village or church to change. They had deliberately chosen to live in an area where they thought that change would be at a minimum. The younger commuting couples or families on the other hand expected a more contemporary response from the church. They tended to be open to change in most areas of their professional life and expected the church to embrace change. He had found that those from the 'lentil and beans' group were often the most suspicious of the church and yet paradoxically the most open to what might more broadly be called religious encounter. For them the church was often perceived as representing an institutional response to religion which they found to be inimical to their own search for a religious dimension to life. His observation was that the original group of village inhabitants were often very pragmatic in their approach to the church. Their major expectation of the church was simply that it should be there, just as it had always been. They could accept change because some change had always taken place, but they often felt pushed out by the newcomers who were both more articulate than they and, certainly in the case of those who had retired, had more time to contribute.

The consequence of such diversity was often that one group tended to dominate, usually not those who had been the original inhabitants. Their response was to drop out of church life, perhaps retaining a commitment to come to the festival occasions and to offer practical help, especially when the church event was more intimately related to a village or community occasion. They continued to look to the church to provide the rites of passage, but regular involvement, especially at a leadership level, was often missing.

While it might be dangerous to build too much on the experience of one man's ministry, his long experience helps to highlight some of the difficult issues that change has brought both to the countryside and to the rural church.

The Small Church in the Inner City

My first ministry was in an inner city church in Birmingham. I well remember one of the older residents in the community telling me that when she was a young girl there were fields between this inner city community and the city centre of Birmingham. At the time I was so surprised that I checked an old map and discovered that she was right. Within one person's lifetime that area had been formally incorporated into the City of Birmingham, had experienced decay among those parts of the housing stock that had been better built, had seen other parts redeveloped completely, most of the older residents had moved out to be replaced by a mix of people who had previously had no contact with the area, and become an area of pressing social need. Change had been rapid, complex and often detrimental.

Large areas of our inner cities represent places where the church has had to attempt to come to terms with the high levels of change that have characterised the community of the inner city. It is often said that in most inner city areas, less than 1% of the population attend any church at all. It should be noted that this generalisation has some notable exceptions. The inner city can be a surprising place! Those inner cities with high levels of immigrants of Irish or Afro-Carribean origin have far higher levels of church attendance than one would normally associate with inner city church life. However, it is true that if one looks only at the indigenous white community one does find very low levels of church attendance. As we indicated in the previous chapter this is not a new phenomenon and was almost certainly true in the previous century when many of the churches now in the inner city were full with middle class and skilled working class people.

Since the Second World War, inner city churches have experienced what, in the United States, has been called 'white flight'. Most middle class people have moved to the newer suburbs and have generally joined churches there. Some, especially those working class people who experienced some improvement in their social standing and who attributed this to their involvement in church life, have continued to commute from suburbia to the inner city churches in which they were brought up and were married. It is very often these commuting Christians who occupy the leadership positions, secretarial and financial, and whose giving keeps the church financially viable. It is also true that the general profile of such commuters is that they are older and thus diminishing as a group.

A good many inner city churches feel beleaguered. Many struggle with large buildings and small, elderly congregations. Even worse, they find that their inner city area has many immigrant peoples whose first language is not English and who worship in new and thriving mosques, guadwaras and temples. There seems to be no point of contact with such newcomers, which throws the mission of that church into question.

These are some of the harsher realities of inner city church life. Yet despite these difficulties, I often find that the church in inner city areas is far from being disconsolate. The period when large numbers of inner city church buildings became redundant is now largely over. Many churches with unmanageably large buildings have had them redeveloped, rebuilt or at least reordered. There are some large and thriving churches in our inner cities and even many of the small inner city churches that I meet often have a sense that there is a new day dawning for church life in these areas of great social need.

I believe that there is a real transition taking place in the life of small inner city churches. The days when they looked back to a large and full church are now so long ago that few can even remember what that was like. The influence of long standing members who commute from the suburbs is often much less. There are increasing signs that the fruit of many dedicated church leaders who have worked very hard for many years without much reward is beginning to emerge. The investment of resource and energy called for by reports such as *Faith in the City* has been made and is beginning to produce benefits. There is an increasing sense that the church is owned by those who live in the inner city and attend these churches. The vision that is beginning to emerge belongs to those for whom the church exists.

This is all encouraging, but there remains one persistent and difficult problem that afflicts any small inner city church that does reach out to its community and sees a response. It doesn't take too long before middle class, often younger, Christians in surrounding suburban areas hear about churches in the inner city that are exhibiting life and growth and who then seek to transfer their membership. These small fires of hope can all too easily be extinguished by the well meaning involvement of those from the suburbs who initially want to support but who, almost despite themselves, end up running everything

The Small Church on the Council Housing Estate

If the church in the inner city has experienced difficulties in the past then the church on Council Housing estates is certainly experiencing problems in the present. The kind of housing estate I have in mind is the kind of large housing project developed since the second World War. These estates, erected so optimistically in the brave new world of the late 1950's, 1960's and early 1970's have almost totally failed to deliver the promise which was contained in their planning. The naive hope that prompted their planning was the notion that if you move people from bad housing stock in deprived inner city areas to communities where the housing is new and is surrounded with areas of green grass, with walkways that separate people from traffic and where new schools and local shops meet local needs, then social problems will largely disappear. The work loads of social workers, probation officers and police departments working in such areas demonstrates the falsity of such hopes. The change that these communities have brought to their residents is not the change that was hoped for, or expected.

Of all the Christians from small churches that I meet in the course of my work, it is those who worship in churches on such housing estates that are the most dispirited. Just as the housing developments themselves were erected in the context of the 'never had it so good' fifties and the 'white hot heat of the technological revolution' sixties, so Christians had high hopes when they caught a vision for the provision of churches on the new estates as they were built. Yet when I meet with the Christians in these churches which were begun with such high hopes twenty and thirty years ago, I meet those who constitute largely the same group of people who were present at the planting of such churches. In very few cases has any real headway been made with local people. Yes, in some cases, a few local people have joined the church, but by and large these are very needy and dependent people who contribute little in terms of leadership and finance. The bulk of the small churches on these estates consist of largely the same people who started them except they are smaller now than they were and are twenty or thirty years older.

What went wrong? When we examine the vision that caused these churches to be started it was almost always the case that Christians in a nearby church saw that a new estate was going to be built and felt strongly that a church should be provided for the new people who would be moving in. The important word in these cases is the word 'provided'. In no case that I know of (and my earnest desire is that someone reading this book will write to me to tell me of one that I don't know of), none of these churches have been started because local Christians on the estate wanted a church and took the initiative to provide one for themselves. The simple fact is that what has been provided has almost always been culturally unsuitable for the people for whom it was intended. These churches have been built, led and financed from outside of the estate and this is where their weakness lies.

I am beginning to hear of very recent attempts to begin Christian work on large council estates that start not with a building or even with public worship. Some groups are concentrating on the kind of relationship building that leads to local people becoming believers and then disciples, meeting initially as small groups in homes before ever coming together to meet for public worship. The shape that such churches take will almost certainly be different to that of the churches which started in buildings at the time when the estates themselves were built. The seriousness of social problems on many of these estates and the almost total failure of the church to make a significant impression on them means that a new start is not just desirable, it is the only way ahead.

The Small Church in the Suburbs

At first sight it might seem that the small church in the suburbs has none of the problems of the first three categories of church we have described. It is rarely wise to be so complacent! The small church in the suburbs is often a pleasant place to be. There is rarely a shortage of finance, there are usually enough volunteers to run the limited programme that is operated, and those in the church have usually been members for a long time and so know each other very well. The Mersey Province of the U.R.C. (a Province which has a very high percentage of small suburban churches), conducted a survey in 1990 which revealed that 69% of their members had been members for more than forty years![9]

There are two important factors which are increasingly affecting the suburban small church which give cause for some concern. The clue to both these factors lies in the observation that many of the members of small suburban churches have belonged for many years. First, there is the fact that suburban life offers choice in almost every area of life. That choice is further increased with the availability of the car. Suburban life offers a very wide range of choice in the area of church life. Evidence from every survey on the subject demonstrates that those under the age of 45 do not consider denomination as a very significant factor in choosing a church. Much more important than denomination is the worship and programme that a church offers. This is especially the case when it comes to the provision of activities for children and youth. Small churches are rarely able to offer a wide range of activities for families. The consequence is that younger families rarely choose to worship at a small church simply because it is close by. Such considerations do not affect those who already worship at a small church. The ties of friendship and familiarity are such that existing worshippers will not exercise the choice available to them by worshipping at a church that offers more activities. However, it does affect the ability of the small suburban church to attract new young families.

The second factor is partly a consequence of the first one, namely that the general profile of small suburban churches indicates that they consist mostly of ageing congregations though often with some children attached, few of whom are from church families. This related factor makes it all the more difficult for such congregations to attract younger adult worshippers. My observation is that small suburban churches often make significant efforts to engage in children's work even though they are not able to offer a full range of family activities. The difficulty is that this work often falls on the shoulders either of those few people in the church who do have young families themselves or on older people who have persevered in such work for many years and feel in need of a break from it. The result can be that children from the community are attracted, but it is much more difficult to persuade the parents of those children to attend events which are not directly related to the children's work itself.

The long term consequence is to place in jeopardy the work with children simply because of the shortage of personnel. Since small churches often look to children's work as a means of providing future recruits, the implication is that this route is increasingly ineffective as a means of ensuring the survival of the small suburban church.

The Small Church in the Small Industrial Town

Some years ago I spent an afternoon with a senior accountant who had worked all of his life in the textile industry. He had recently retired and he told me that most of his professional life had been spent closing textile mills. In the area where he lived there was then only one mill left out of the hundreds that had existed at the start of his working life and even that mill was unlikely to survive. Whether it worked with cotton, or knitwear or shoemaking, virtually every small industrial town has changed out of all recognition over the past half century. Many have found new prosperity in quite different industries. Some, such as a town like Skipton, have benefited from the tourist industry; others have become centres for white collar commerce centred on the insurance, banking or building society industries. But few, if any, small towns have escaped change and radical change at that.

Much of the church life that existed when these small towns were at the height of their industrial activity echoed the wealth that was created by those same industries. The church buildings erected in the 19th century bore the hallmarks of the patronage of the then newly wealthy industrialists, many of whom attended church themselves and earnestly hoped that their workers would follow their example. The division between church and chapel was acute and reflected something of the divisions in society as a whole. At the height of their success the churches and chapels of the industrial small town reflected the culture of those towns to an astonishing degree.

Of all the types of small church one has the feeling that small churches in this situation reflect, in the words of one minister, 'a great future behind us'. Past glories rather than a happy present seem to dominate such churches far more than the atmosphere of inner city congregations where something of the same reality was once at work. I have sometimes been surprised at the degree to which the worship, the building in all its glorious detail (and not such glorious leaking roofs), and programme reflect a culture which has long since gone. The small church in such situations seems to have coped with change by ignoring it as much as possible. The consequence of such unchanging cultural values is very often that new people have great difficulty in breaking in to such structures. It is almost as if such churches are not only asking potentially new Christians to believe that Jesus Christ is the Son of God, that he was crucified and raised from the dead, but also to express that faith in a culture that has not really been expressive of movements in society since the 1930's. That is very hard to do when you were born after the Second World War. Incredibly, some, although very few, have managed it!

The Reality of the Single Cell Unit

What is at work in all of these situations is a degree of tension produced by the reality of the church as a single cell unit.

Whenever there is the need, such as in the case of the small rural church, for more than one significant group to be ministered to, there is a danger of one group becoming dominant at the expense of all the other groups. This ensures that the small church remains a single cell organisation but it reduces the possibility of the church reaching out beyond a single group. In the case of some other churches, for example those in the inner city and the council housing estate, the dominance of those of other social groups who come from outside of the immediate area prevents the emergence of a single celled group from within the community that is being served. The church in the suburbs and church in the small town, for quite different reasons, maintains a single celled existence but by so doing threatens their own future.

This issue will need to be taken up again in part three of this book which deals with strategy. For the moment it is enough to say that it is necessary for the small church in these situations to facilitate the development of a culture or identity that will be able to transcend the various groups that need to characterise such churches, but which will still result in the emergence of a single celled organisation.

Notes

1. Roger Jowell, Lindsay Brook, Gillian Prior and Bridget Taylor (Eds), *British Social Attitudes: The Ninth Report, Social and Community Planning Research*, (Dartmouth Publishing: 1992), p 55 claims that 69% of people in Britain believe in God; p 56 claims that 64% of people in Britain are affiliated to a denomination; p 60 claims that 58% of people have either complete, a great deal of or some confidence in the churches.
2. Adrian Hastings, *A History of English Christianity 1920–1990*, (S.C.M.: London, 1991), p xxvii.
3. Alvin Toffler, *Future Shock*, (Pan Books: London, 1970), p 22.
4. David Holloway, *Ready Steady Grow: Principles for the growth of the church in Britain*, (Kingsway: Eastbourne, 1989), p 93.

5. Andrew Greeley writing in Roger Jowell, Lindsay Brook, Gillian Prior and Bridget Taylor (Eds), *British Social Attitudes: The Ninth Report*, *Social and Community Planning Research*, (Dartmouth Publishing: 1992), p 52.
6. *Faith in the Countryside*: Report of the Archbishops' Commission on Rural Areas, (Acora Publishing: Stoneleigh Park, 1990), p 2.
7. *Ibid* p 23.
8. *Ibid* p 309.
9. Report in *Reform*: September 1988.

CHAPTER FOUR

WHO ATTENDS THE SMALL CHURCH?

Imagine for a moment a situation where a family moves into a new community, a small town of some 15,000 people. They are practising Christians and now that they are in their new home they begin to look for a church. The mother and father both work outside of the home and both have careers in the professions. They have three children between the ages of ten and sixteen.

In the immediate community there are seven churches. Two of these churches are far removed from the kind of churchmanship that they have been used to and they would have some doctrinal difficulties attending either of these two churches. That leaves five churches, which although they are all of different denominations, the family would feel broadly happy with. Out of these five churches, two have an attendance of under thirty people, one is attended by around sixty people and of the remaining two churches, one has a regular attendance of 120 people and the remaining church 300 people.

If you were to be asked to guess which of these churches would the family be most likely to visit first, and which of these churches would they be most likely to settle in, I wonder what your reply would be. My suspicion is that most people who read these words would expect the family that we have described to visit the two churches with an attendance of more than one hundred and if they felt comfortable with one of these churches to settle in one of them. An intrepid explorer might venture as far as the church with sixty in attendance, but few of us would expect this particular family to visit both of the small churches in the town.

Why is it that we would expect matters to work in this way? Why should we not expect that a new family in town would want to begin by exploring the smaller churches where presumably they would receive a warmer welcome and indeed be able to make a more significant contribution? A family of five coming into a church of under thirty would have the potential to transform the situation. Now of course, no-one is ruling out the possibility that a new family would begin by visiting and then joining one of the smaller churches in the town, but it just isn't what we would expect to happen. Moreover, there are some very good reasons as to why our expectations are shaped in this particular way.

First, it is rarely the case that families, no matter how committed, see it as their call to transform a new church just because they have moved home. That is not the first item on their agenda. Secondly, such a family will probably be concerned to ensure that there are activities for their children and that their children will be able to meet other Christian young people. Thirdly, it is very likely that a family will be looking for a quality in the total experience of worship that most of us realise is rarely present in the small church. In fact if we allow our imaginations to paint a picture of what such a family might find in both the churches with attendances of under thirty, we might be likely to conclude that it would take a very special kind of person to even undertake a visit.

In other words, it seems to be the case that it is the larger churches which tend to attract those who are in the professions, who are well educated and who have significant levels of ability. This can be deeply frustrating for the members and leaders of small churches who are often anxious to have stable new people with ability join their church. Especially since they reason that the nearby large church already has many such people and doesn't really need anymore in order to fulfil its mission. But it is important to be realistic about what the situation actually is rather than to waste too much time and effort lamenting that it is not somehow different.

This does not mean that there is never anyone of ability in a small church. What it does mean is that those who join small churches tend to do so for one, or a combination of more than one, very particular reason. If we can understand what those reasons are we can build up a profile of the various kinds of people that join the small church.

Those Who Join the Small Church

The family member

One church that I knew well had been known for many years as the 'Smith church'. This was not a new kind of cult but simply a reflection of the fact that the other church members and the community had recognised the dominance of one particular family in the life of that church. At one time the church had been led by a strong lay leader who had seven sons and one daughter. That one family dictated the pattern of church life for three generations, almost one hundred years in total. Even such matters as the acceptable menu for a church social was shaped by the custom of a matriarchal figure whose love of pickled onions influenced the smell of that small church for decades!

But, as we mentioned in Chapter Two, important as family membership has been in the past, it is markedly less so now. A very high percentage of young people brought up in Christian families leave home to study at University or College. The figure for Christian families is much higher than the average for the population as a whole. It is not very often that those same young people will return to their home town to find employment and a settled future. The absence of a continuing flow of future leaders from key families already in the church has brought something of a crisis for many small churches anxious to locate leaders. One still does find family members returning to their home church, but it is no longer the single most important source of continuing leadership recruitment.

Those who value the small group

A survey among those who attended Spring Harvest in 1993 reported a very high percentage of people attending a small group within their church. Clearly this is not a group of people that is representative of the whole church but it does indicate that a large number of Christians value the experience of the small group.[1] Other figures compiled a few years ago estimated that more than a million Christians meet in weekly small group studies of one kind or another. There are clearly many people other than those who attend small churches who value the experience of the small group.

For a time, I worked on the staff of a church with a book membership of 1500. The senior minister of that church was fond of saying, 'We can only be a large church because we also know how to be a small church'. His comment was a reflection of the caring role of their effective small group programme. Others who have undertaken research on why people leave churches have indicated that unless a person has six or more friends in a church after six months it is unlikely that they will remain in that church.[2]

Clearly many people enjoy the intimacy of relationships that come with belonging to a small group. But some who belong to small churches do so because they are looking for something more than just membership of a small group. For them it is important to be able to know everyone in the church personally. The small church acts like a large house group or an extended family. Such a person can feel uncomfortable if the church grows to the point where it would not be possible to greet everyone who attends the regular worship service.

Those who need high levels of care

Small churches are often very caring places to be. People rather than task is one of the very strong characteristics of the small church. The natural consequence is that many small churches contain a high percentage of people who need a great deal of care, especially if the kind of care that they seek is attention as compared with specialist counselling.

The tendency for small churches to contain high percentages of needy people is a very mixed blessing. Some Christian leaders observe that it is only realistic for a church to care for needy people on a ratio of ten stable people to one who is in need. It is not uncommon for the ratio of needy people to be somewhat higher than this in a small church. This single factor can sometimes seriously impede the growth potential of the small church. It can also be argued that some of the emotionally damaged people in a small church receive a great deal of attention, but not actual healing. In other words, the very fact of receiving attention sometimes exacerbates a problem rather than helps it.

In some cases, the leaders of small churches will know the pain of having helped people through to recovery only to find that those same people leave the church for a larger church once they are through their immediate crisis. Just as painful is the discovery that needy people will sometimes resist the growth of the small church. Should a small church begin to grow then those who are very needy people will either get better or leave to join another very small church.

Those with a strong commitment to particular values

Although commitment to a particular denomination and to no other, is nowhere near as strong today as it once was, there are still those people who will have such a strong commitment to a particular denomination that this one factor will outweigh all others. So, for example, if the fictional family we described at the beginning of this chapter had a strong denominational commitment, then that commitment might override other considerations in choosing a church to join. They might previously have been members of a large church elsewhere and from a socio-economic perspective been more comfortable in a large church of another denomination. Yet their particular allegiance to, and involvement in, their denomination might take precedence over these other considerations.

Such a phenomenon is not restricted only to the issue of denomination. The same process could also apply in such matters as worship style or congregational ethos. I have certainly known those people who have been part of a congregation with, for example, a strong sense of the value of personal relationships who, having moved home, have looked for another church which, regardless of denomination or size, would contain some or all of those same values.

Those who have a strong sense of mission

There are those individuals who make a conscious choice concerning their church allegiance on the basis of the service that they can offer. Such people may be motivated by a number of factors to join a small church, not necessarily because it is small but because it meets one or more of the mission criteria that they have in mind. First, they may have strong convictions about the need to be a part of a church in their immediate community. The nearest church to where they live might happen to be a small church, but from their perspective this would be the most appropriate place in which to express their service to Christ.

Secondly, there might be a particular aspect or project sponsored by a particular church which captures their imagination. It may be that a nearby small church has a strong commitment to a programme for offenders, or some other needy social group, that coincides with their own area of interest.

Thirdly, a strong sense of commitment to an issue such as racial justice, or a commitment to the poor might cause someone with a strong sense of mission to either travel some distance, or deliberately move home to work with a small church that was seeking to tackle such issues on the 'front-line' of mission. A good number of inner city churches have been greatly strengthened through the years by the involvement of such highly committed individuals.

Fourthly, it may well be the perception of a highly motivated person that a particular church needs the gifts that they have to offer. Again, I have known people who have deliberately moved from a large church, often with the blessing of that congregation, in order to make a distinct and identifiable contribution to the life of a needy small church. Clearly those who are motivated in such a way will not be planning to sit on the back seat of the church, and because of their particular commitment will not be greatly worried by what others might see as the disadvantages of the small church. Indeed it is often those very supposed problems that act as a motivational stimulus.

The above is not intended to be an exhaustive list of all those who might attend the small church in preference to any other size of church, but what we do see in these types of person is a very interesting combination of personal commitment to service with a strong sense of the value of relationship. Sometimes one person only exhibits a strong sense of service while others might only see the value of relationships, but the overall team that is built will clearly demonstrate a strong combination of both. It is this combination which often ensures that the small church survives against the odds.

The Team that is the Small Church

The strong sense of family that emerges from the combination of members we have just described produces a strong sense that the small church comprises a single team. Eddie Gibbs, writing in his book *I Believe in Church Growth* confirms very strongly this sense of team when describing the particular management style exhibited by the primary leader of a small church.

> In a small church with a membership of up to say sixty five, the management style of the leader will probably be at the level of team leader or charge hand. They are one of a work team who are able to stand in for any of the members. They are available to be personally involved in every task which comes to hand.[3]

Given the particular profile of those who attend the small church, the question for such a team will be, how do these types of people fit together in such a way that the church can be a healthy team? A leader in the Congregational Federation, (a denomination with a large number of small churches), Graham Adams, has conducted a highly original piece of unpublished research on the management styles of teams in church life.[4] Although Adams did not have the small church especially in mind when conducting his research, his findings are highly applicable in this setting. His detailed analysis of the leadership teams of four churches used the Belbin method of categorising team members. Belbin's team categories are as follows:

1. The Company Worker

This would be the person who '. . . works for the church, rather than the pursuit of self-interest and does so in a practical and realistic way. In short, he is someone who can readily identify with the organisation.'[5] This team worker takes a servant attitude towards jobs that may be very uninteresting routine tasks. They are willing helpers.

2. The Team Worker

There is not a huge difference between the team worker and the company worker. The added dimension though is that the team worker is often a 'peacemaker' whose contribution helps to bring harmony to the team relationship. They are sensitive people who have a strong interest in the needs of others in the team.

3. The Completer-Finisher

The term 'completer-finisher' describes very well the main characteristics of this team member. Attention to detail features prominently in the profile of this participant. Interestingly, Adams refers to Belbin and Harston's discovery that those who have a completer-finisher approach have a very high sense of obligation in relation to the task. They are high in self discipline and self control. Adams comments that these are qualities that are often taught in church life as being necessary for Christian living.

4. The Chairman

A good team leader often has the attributes of the chairman. The chairman is someone who is able to affirm others and encourage them to fulfil their task, while at the same time having a strong commitment to the ongoing task that the group is attempting to achieve. Adam's notes that in his research the minister was often expected to be the chairman but none of the four ministers in his study scored highly as chairman!

5. The Shaper

Beware! Those who are shapers are often prone to irritation and impatience. Ironically it is these very qualities which are the side effect of that which makes shapers so helpful in a team situation. The shaper is someone who is impatient with the situation as it is. They want to bring change and will often galvanise support for bringing an improvement to a situation. Adams comments, 'The Shaper almost always makes a positive impact.'[6]

6. The Plant

No team can cope with too many Plants within the team—one is often enough! To quote Adams: 'Plants are usually individualistic, serious-minded and unorthodox. They possess imagination, intellect and knowledge, but are often inclined to disregard practical details or protocol. The evidence suggests the importance of having a Plant in each team'[7]

7. The Resource Investigator

In Belbin's model, the Resource Investigator is a very similar character to that of the Plant, but unlike the Plant they are much more 'team' or 'people oriented' in their personality. They like to see how best they can use resources, particularly the gifts of others, in the development of the project. As the term suggests, they like to extract information which they feel will be helpful to the situation. One definition quoted by Adams is that 'he is an executive who is never in his room and if he is, he is on the 'phone.'[8]

8. The Monitor-Evaluator

Those who we might describe as Monitor-Evaluators contribute the ability to assess the various options on offer and make a good recommendation as to the relative merits of particular proposals. Adams suggest that: 'Such a task requires a person who possesses a high level of mental activity combined with disinterested detachment. . . . Usually he is a person with low drive. The Monitor-Evaluator often appears a rather dry, boring and overcritical person.'[9]

Belbin's method of assessing the contribution of people to team situations, as with all other such systems, needs to be treated carefully. First, it needs to be said that no one person fits into any of these categories exactly. Some people may overlap with two or three such tendencies depending on the precise situation in which thay find themselves. Second, no description such as Belbin's adequately conveys the whole of a person's contribution to a team or a church. These are only helpful tools in understanding what tends to work and what tends to fail. They do not map cast iron certainties.

Bearing in mind these important qualifications, what can we learn about church life and more particularly, small church life? The research of Graham Adams clearly shows that the teams he investigated had a high proportion of Company Workers, Team Workers and Completer Finishers. Those who are observers of the church scene would hardly be surprised by such a finding. Interestingly, Adams argues that there is something about the values of the Christian community that tends to encourage people with those characteristics and which conversely tends not to attract those with a stronger individualistic and innovative contribution.[10]

However, the problem is that a successful team, according to the Belbin model, does need to have some who are Plants, Chairmen, Resource-Investigators, Shapers and Monitor-Evaluators. Of these, one needs at least a strong Shaper and either a Plant or a Resource Investigator. While agreeing with Adams that the church often does lack these latter categories of people, I would suggest that the reasons for this go deeper than simply the existence of more corporate values within the Christian church. Many, if not most churches, are concerned today with maintenance as compared to mission, and I would suggest that it would require a much stronger 'mission motif' to be able to draw those who might contribute the innovative and creative cutting edge to church life. Even more problematic is the fact that the standing of the church in society means that it is often those with the greatest ability, the opinion formers, the leaders, who are not found in church. Thus, even those churches who do have a vision for mission are often attempting to engage in that mission with teams that are dominated by those who are Company Workers, Team Members and Completer Finishers.

The small church is perhaps even more likely to attract those who are in this category of the Company Workers, Team Members and Completer Finishers. This tendency is enhanced by the various factors that we noted earlier in this chapter concerning those who attend the small church. Those who are needy, who demonstrate the need for some degree of dependence, those who are more compliant in their attitude are drawn to smaller churches and tend to also fall into this category.

The consequence of such a situation can be fatal for a small church. The outcome is often a self-perpetuating cycle of stagnation. The lack of movement tends to alienate even those people of ability who are in the small church; the lack of people with a creative contribution tends to produce stagnation. That then raises a key question, from what source can a small church obtain at least some of the input that comes from those who are Shapers and either Plants or Resource- Investigators? We will attempt to suggest at least one solution to this dilemma in Chapter Thirteen.

Notes

1. The Spring Harvest research reported that 79% of respondents met regularly in a small group which included some Bible study.
2. See research contained in the book by Alan F Harre, *Close the Back Door*, (Concordia: 1984).
3. Eddie Gibbs, *I Believe in Church Growth*, (Hodder and Stoughton: London, Updated Edition 1990), p 260.
4. Graham M Adams, Unpublished thesis submitted for a Masters Degree in Business Administration at Leicester Polytechnic, 1985.
5. *Ibid* p 31.
6. *Ibid* p 34.
7. *Ibid* p 34f.
8. *Ibid* p 35.
9. *Ibid* p 36.
10. *Ibid* p 44.

CHAPTER FIVE

IDENTIFYING THE SMALLER CHURCH

I completed my theological training in the beginning years of the 1980's. Those ten years gave rise to many new trends: economically it was the growth of materialism; politically it was the Thatcherite years; musically the advent of punk and new wave. Changes and growth were evident in many places, including the church. In the midst of this decade a new value, the rise of the megachurch, was to affect the outlook of discussions on the church. The beginning of the 1990's has not significantly altered this perspective.

With the rise of the largest[1], what will become of the small and the smallest, once held to be beautiful?[2] The Western culture within which we live revels in juxtapositions. So in the midst of change and growth, the small and the compact are deemed equally important and welcome. Compact discs, personal stereos, smaller cars, all seem to be advantageous to our lives. Thank you micro chip!

Because of this sense of juxtaposition between the large and the small, how do we treat the relative values which are attached to the concepts of each? The standards of assumption can be the same for both. The small and compact is often seen as a reduced version of the larger. Nothing is lost in either quality or performance. And in the world of electronics and computer games, this may be relatively true.

But in the places of personal relationships, community activities, and indeed the church, this is far from a correct perspective. Sociologically, with the demise of both community and family as larger units, much of the networks of support, strength, and acceptability have been lost. We are now individuals located in small nuclear and single families surrounded by hundreds of people deemed 'neighbours' by our culture. We often do not speak to each other, know one another's names, or have any significant conversations with one another outside of the weather. Small, in this context, is neither better nor welcome. Loneliness, despair, and nihilism are often characteristic of our world, and Western civilisation in particular.

This is certainly true in America. Os Guinness, while offering a very poignant and penetrating analysis of religion and social reality in the States, offers this comment with regard to the problem of homelessness:

> Aloneness breeds loneliness and loneliness breeds alienation. A culture of separation has become the norm. Modern individuals are on their own. Each in a crucial sense is more and more stuck with himself or herself. The search for self is the mooring of the last resort. When that, too, gives way, the crisis that begins with the specific aches and pains of battered selves ends with an overwhelming longing to be all of a piece.[3]

The larger community and the smaller family are each unique. While in the larger group, the individual is valued, in smaller groups, the need for community and the sense of family are vital.[4]

The church of Jesus Christ brings a message of welcome news. Any church which is faithful to the gospel will proclaim that message in its life and work in every community. Unfortunately, the values of our culture have also infiltrated our places of worship as well. We often now assume that large is best, and more importantly for our purposes, that the large and small church are identical in every way except size. Is this a valid assumption?

My family and I began ministering in the 1980's. Our training and practical experience were with larger churches, but we were led to work with a church of 5 adults and a handful of children. We had unknowingly entered the world of the small church. But how do we work with the small church? We needed some help.

One American author has done more to help the readers and

leaders of smaller churches understand and adapt to the distinctives of their life and worship than any other. His name is Lyle Schaller. He is the author of numerous books; the editor of Abingdon Press' Creative Leadership Series; a parish consultant with the Yokefellow Institute in Richmond, Indiana, USA; and has worked over the years with a significant number and variety of churches across the United States and Canada listening, studying, probing and reflecting on the small church.[5]

In his celebrated book, *The Small Church is Different*,[6] Schaller identifies 20 differences between the smaller church and other churches. In this chapter, we want to examine seven of these differences in detail and compare the ways in which they relate to our experiences of the small church in the UK.[7]

The Small Church is Tough!

Ask any minister or church leader about the resilience of the smaller church and you will most assuredly find both a smile and a look of frustration on their face- sometimes at the same time! There is no question that churches which are smaller are also tough. They seem to be able to weather any storm and keep on going- especially the storm of change.

Some of that toughness is both necessary and commendable. Within the local communities where churches find themselves, there will have been great social and economic changes in the past few decades. Those churches which have continued to be faithful in their proclamation of the gospel in addition to their very presence as the body of Christ locally, are often one of the few areas of stability in this rapidly changing environment.

The other side of the coin, however, is that churches which are tough are also usually resistant to change, to adaptation, and so to growth. The perseverance of the faithful few is often echoed in the battle cry, 'This is our church'; 'This is the way we have always done it'; 'I remember when . . .' These and other such statements indicate the tenacity and non- flexibility of the smaller church to look realistically at itself and the world around it.

This same toughness which keeps the doors open and the church going also keeps the outsider outside. Saying the small church is tough does not indicate a resistance to be uncaring. On the contrary, one of the small church's greatest assets is the level of care which is provided to all who belong. Of course, for the outsider, they face the dilemma of not belonging, hence it seems to them that this church doesn't care, it is not interested in them. But care is given primarily within the group, and the small church knows its own.

In an important paper[8] which faces some of the issues relating to this and other salient points, Carl S. Dudley points out that the small church has as its raison d'être the ability to know each person in the congregation face to face. Larger churches do not carry this value in their ethos. In a rapidly changing and mobile culture, the value of personal encounter is vital. Larger churches usually tackle this area with small groups of some description.[9] However, according to Dudley, the preference of the small church to have face to face encounters can give the impression to both outsider as well as church member that the church is full up.[10] No further personal involvement can take place, because all the relationships most people can maintain are already in existence.

It is precisely here that the small church must adjust itelf. But how does the unwelcoming guardian of tradition offer hands of friendship to newcomers? And how does the toughness of the small church give way to the open doors of caring beyond the primary group?[11]

The Importance of Lay Ministry

Since the days of the Reformation at least, the concept of the 'priesthood of all believers' has been the cry and suggested model for church ministry. The reality, in many larger churches, has often been different. In contrast, for the small church, the involvement of the laity in ministry is the normal expression. In many churches both in the US and the UK, the work of the laity has overshadowed any significant and long-term involvement of the pastor or clergy. Some denominations have insisted that lay ministry is the only appropriate method (for e.g., the Brethren).

Frequently, small churches cannot adequately finance full-time or even part-time trained leadership. In addition, these same churches expect and need a high involvement from their membership.[12] This is the case regardless of any particular theological understanding of ministry or leadership. Small churches simply could not continue to survive in the day to day running of the church without the active involvement of many of its lay members.

The obvious advantage of this situation is that there are relatively few pew warmers. Everyone has a part to play, and each part is valued in light of the overall whole. At least that is the suggested theory. However, in my experience there can still be an unstated but recognised hierarchy of ministry gifts which are deemed most important, along with an equally unstated list of who is entitled to participate in their expression.[13] At any rate, the model of the church as the body of Christ is for the small church the most appropriate if not the only example of how the church should function.

There are of course difficulties when lay ministry is valued so highly. One obvious problem is the place of trained ministers and leaders. Since they are often not part of the original community where the church is located, they are outsiders in two senses. They are separated by their origins as well as by their training. So the leaders, unless they are readily accepted and adapt to the new commmunity where the church is located, find it difficult to understand and move the church forward in growth. Feelings of frustration, loneliness, disappointment, lack of vision, questions of calling; all can be part of the emotional baggage of trained leaders in small churches. Schaller reminds us that the small church resists the leadership of trained ministers.[14]

In addition to this, Dudley has rightly pointed out that the large church requires *specialists* for the job of moving and building the church; the pastor of the medium-sized church must be a *generalist*, who has some expertise in many areas; but the pastor of the small church is primarily a *lover*.[15] This area of leadership, both trained and lay, will be dealt with more specifically in chapters six and seven. Here we want to highlight that there are peculiar tensions between the lay and trained elements in the small church.

There are, of course, exceptions to this scenario. In particular, Schaller has noted three in the North American context which we can easily adapt to life in the UK church. These are: 1) the new church (church plant) which is still being served by the original pastor. Here, the development of vision, friendship, and understanding are all more or less equal in the church; 2) black and ethnic churches in general, which tend to have a strong pastor-centred approach to ministry; and 3) churches which are independent (ie, non-denominational, FIEC [Fellowship of Independent Evangelical Churches], as well as denominations which include autonomous congregations), or those which are at the very conservative or very liberal ends of the theological spectrum. Here the issues are often related to the 'authority' of the minister or leader, as much as to the working dynamic of the church.[16]

There is no question that lay minstry is crucial for all church life, and the small church regularly counts the cost of its life and ministry by the active involvement and participation of its lay ministry. But the tensions between trained clergy and lay leadership, the use and value of each type, must be faced for the church to move forward for growth.

A Volunteer Organisation

Anyone who knows anything about American culture will soon realise that the characteristic of voluntarism is part and parcel of that society. This factor is no less prominent within the structures of the church. By a 'volunteer organisation', Schaller is here contrasting the prominence in larger churches of paid staff for various duties and ministries (youth work, worship leader, maintenance), whereas in the smaller church which cannot afford to do this, a volunteer base is used to staff these various ministries.[17]

In Britain, even though we might not always think in these

particular terms, in practice this type of procedure is often emulated in the smaller church. A particular job needs to be done (flower rotas, Sunday School teachers, visiting members) and so we ask people to fill the gap—often without due consideration of their giftedness, calling and temperament.[18]

The changes in our society have also added complications to the ministry of the small church. Every group from the political party to the local community organisation is experiencing tremendous frustration with the need for helpers. But they seem to be in short supply. This presents a difficult challenge to the small church, which must locate those members who are willing and able to keep the church going, and the doors open.

So here are two challenges for the smaller church: finding enough available people as well as the right (gifted) ones. The response of the smaller church to this challenge will undoubtedly reflect the ethos of the changing social structures. Whereas the larger church will have greater resources and staff at its disposal, the smaller church's contribution must not be over-looked or considered irrelevant. Helping people discover their gifts and finding ways of expressing these is potentially a simpler task for the small single-celled churches. Here love, care and commitment are often felt more deeply and therefore trust can be more easily established. The small church must learn to be content with a few areas of ministry which are done well with adequate staff, rather than attempting to succumb to the pressures of trying to provide more than it is able.

People Matter More Than Performance

One concept which can be used to describe the larger American (and other Western) church experience is professional quality. The public performance aspect of worship is evidenced in such specialist expressions as paid choir singers, music leaders, radio and TV ministries, the dominant position of the clergy in the service, and even the type of liturgy which is used. Of course, for the smaller church this is either unobtainable or anathema, depending upon one's perspective.

This does not mean, however, that smaller churches are any

less concerned with the quality of their ministry. They are equally as conscientious. They will work as hard with less resources and staff than the larger church. But overall, for worshippers in smaller churches, the issues of intimacy and involvement are generally much more important considerations.[19]

In the recent film 'Sister Act', female actress Whoopi Goldberg's role as a nightclub singer posing as a nun in hiding who initiates change is a helpful way of illustrating this tension between the small and large church and its members. In the film, the church choir was regularly called upon to sing in Sunday worship services. Being part of the choir had much more to do with being part of the group than whether anyone could actually sing–or at least sing well. The vast empty church with a few faithful parishioners seated here and there demonstrated that people mattered most. But once Miss Goldberg gained control of directing the choir, the focus changed from person to performance and professional quality. Now the church soon begins to fill up, and the choir–astute in their musical renditions, have become the centrepiece of this dying church. Whoopi packs them in, getting 'butts on seats' in her words. It's not that people no longer matter, but the aim has now shifted towards presentation rather than participation. In the film, the small dying church has now become a large growing concern.

A number of observers of the smaller church have commented that one of the greatest assets it possesses is its intimacy: the face-to-face relationships with individual members.[20] This has been evidenced many times in my ministry within the small church. The informality, the notation, either mentally or aloud, of who is present and who is missing (so the church is incomplete); all this and much more indicates one of the strengths of the small church. The danger is that when the church does begin to grow and new people are added (or new initiatives and approaches to worship are experienced, or even a more professional attitude to the church's work is expressed), a gap has been created whereby the people can begin to feel that they no longer matter to the church. A sense of belonging must be maintained.

Meetings, Tasks, and People

The way that the small church involves people, performs tasks, and holds meetings is expressed quite uniquely. There are three particular expressions which need to be considered.

Committees versus individuals

Committees and meetings are often the bane of many churches. Yet, in larger churches, there is no better method of achieving what needs to be done than to have a group of committed individuals working together for the benefit of the church. Larger churches cannot afford the luxury of time and personal involvement by every member on every decision. Hence there are often specific areas which are delegated and managed by committees or leaders (such as worship, administration, pastoral work, office work, and evangelism).

In small churches, along with the absence of numerous committee structures (even though there are obviously exceptions to this observation), specific individuals will be key to seeing that the required job gets done. In fact, within some small churches, this is the only way that is acceptable to proceed. The minister is often this key person in small churches, despite the fact that his leadership is resisted. He becomes the organiser, the one who shares the ideas, and the one who gets stuck with getting the job done. Delegation, and perhaps more importantly, responsible people who will complete the task, are mere dreams in the reality of being all things to all needs.

The small church is often a participatory democracy

Schaller's description has much more meaning for North American congregations where the combination of participation (volunteering) and democracy (everyone having their say) is strongly valued, especially in the small church. However, his overall observation is consistent with the UK situation.

Larger churches operate with authority being vested in a few key leaders, whereas smaller churches are almost inevitably congregational in decision making, and this often with little regard to their connections of denomination or network. The obvious exception to this is perhaps some of the house church networks, which tend to have a stronger authority structure. But even here, my observation is that if they are smaller churches, they will tend to focus on the local congregation more so than the national network.

Social meetings dominate the agenda of the small church

With a larger church, efficiency is vital. As a general rule, every meeting is conducted with the prime focus on getting through the agenda within the suggested limits of time. The understanding here is that the 'business' of the church must be done effectively and efficiently. So the stated agenda is the primary focus.

In small churches, even though there may be an agenda for business, the social element is at least as vital to the meeting, or even perhaps more so. A ninety minute meeting in a large church might be a three hour meeting in a smaller church, by the time people have shared personally with each other, partaken of refreshments, and finally attended to the business at hand. Equally, the focus is often on particular details whereas in the larger church, the emphasis might be more on broad policy decisions in such meetings.

The large and small church are both involved in church business. But the focal point in each is slightly different. As stated above, the larger church functions primarily as an organisation whereas the smaller church is an organism. Within the small church, the way in which the job is done is as important as getting the job done.

A Majority of Small Churches are Subsidised

Schaller helpfully points out two ways in which nearly all churches, especially smaller ones are not really paying their own way.

First, the church which meets in a building erected by a previous generation of believers is obviously subsidised by past giving. This is also true of the land, the parsonage or manse, and the internal furnishings.

Secondly, many small churches, especially those connected with older denominations, are not expected to pay for their minister's salary directly. There is usually some governing board for the allocation of monies, otherwise this church could not have full-time or even part-time Christian leadership. This is equally true in some churches where monies are paid from outside the country of work, by a mission board, or other church network, often until such time as the local congregation can pay their own way. This is also relevant in the early years of many church planting ventures.

A third way, not specifically mentioned by Schaller, but none-the-less important in the life of the smaller church, is the subsidy of prayer. This, of course, is also true for the larger church, but for many small churches with a life history of many hundreds of years, this is no small matter. The faithfulness and perseverance of the saints throughout the decades (and in some cases centuries) has enabled this present group of believers to meet and function as a church today. We cannot begin to calculate the importance of this, nor should we try. The spiritual heritage and history of each church is a further subsidy which must not be overlooked.[21]

Of course the observant reader and leader is aware that all churches are subsidised to some degree or another. But today's small churches must face the tasks and opportunities afforded to them with a present expression of faith- no matter how small that may seem. As with the mustard seed in Luke 13, even a small faith can produce great fruit.

Evangelism: 'Attraction' Versus Proclamation

Schaller, following the observations of McGavran and Arn, notes that there are broadly two New Testament models for church evangelism.

The first of these is the proclamation model. In this approach, the church is actively involved in going out and reaching people with the claims of Jesus as Lord and Saviour, reaching people outside the door of its own fellowship. Therefore, a variety of means are used in order to evangelise the unchurched, such as door-to-door outreach, open air services, and even quality worship and preaching. This is the predominant expression of the larger church.

The smaller church operates primarily on the attraction model. This passive expression might include listing the service times on the notice board (including any special events like Harvest Suppers or guest missionaries), publishing the church services regularly in the local newspaper, assuming members will naturally invite their unchurched friends and family who are not Christians to these events. This approach assumes that those outside the doors of the church will be naturally 'attracted' to the life of the church and want to join.

There are of course some obvious reasons for the distinction between the variety of approaches taken by larger and smaller churches. First, very often the smaller church has limited resources, hence can rarely focus on outward, proclamation evangelism. Secondly, the tensions of assimilating new people can be very difficult for the smaller church, especially if there is a large influx. This would upset the balance of the present group dynamics which are often offering security for the current members. Thirdly, where small churches do change their tactics and consciously begin to use the proclamation model, they often cease to remain as small churches as they begin to experience growth.

One of the most significant tasks facing the future of the small church is in answering the question—how do we initiate and achieve the movement from small to large(r)? At the very least, points of entry as compared to programmed evangelism are pivotal for the longevity of the small church. Some growth is essential or the church will ultimately cease to exist.

In the book of Acts, the problem of taking the gospel to all the nations was effectively initiated by active persecution which caused the gathered congregation to scatter and spread. Perhaps this is one of the reasons why the church is substantially growing in places of poverty and persecution.

Equally this may have something to do with the current (though not new) observation that church planting is the best method under heaven for the church to grow. The church is scattered until it settles. The dynamic of movement is in the forefront, prior to stability. Later chapters will help to assist the small church in facing the opportunities for growth, as well as helping to tackle the issue of motivation for mission.

In all the above named differences between the large church and the smaller, we are very grateful to Lyle Schaller for indicating in such a penetrating way these distinctions. Most readers who have ever been involved with small churches will readily identify with many, if not most, of the seven mentioned descriptions out of the twenty that Schaller offers.

This identification process helps us to understand, in a more penetrating way, the value as well as the limitations of the smaller church. But we are still painting a picture with rather broad strokes. We have occasionally noted above that there are obvious exceptions to many of these descriptive analyses. It is now time to begin painting a more detailed picture in looking at some of the particular issues which face the small church.

Notes

1. On the related issues of mega trends, see the important book *Mega Trends* by John Nasbitt (Sidgwick & Jackson: London, 1982) and more recently *Mega Trends 2000* by John Nasbitt and Patricia Aberdene (Sidgwick & Jackson: London, 1990).

2. See the important book *Small is Beautiful* by E F Schumacher (Abacus: 1973).

3. Os Guinness *The American Hour* (The Free Press: New York, 1993), p 310.

4. Perhaps this is one explanation for the proliferation of secluded religious groups and the recent catastrophe at Waco with David Koresh and the Branch Davidians in Waco, Texas.

5. It is important to note two particular variances with Schaller's work and this one. First, Schaller assumes a church which has less than 200 members is small. Our assumption is that any church which has less than 50 regular worshippers is small.

Secondly, when Schaller first authored his book, the normal sized North American Protestant congregation was 40 in worship attendance.

Statistically, the average size church in the UK and the US is now considered by some church growth people to be 70 members. But of course, the discerning reader will quickly note that the spiritual environment between the States and the UK is significantly different. See the results of the survey in *Church Growth Digest Year 14*, Issue 2 (Winter 1992/93), p 6 by Andrew Greeley.

6. Lyle Schaller, *The Small Church is Different* (Abingdon Press: Nashville, 1982). The reader might also be interested to read another of Schaller's works which makes other significant contributions to our understanding of the smaller church. See Schaller, *Activating the Passive Church* (Abingdon Press: Nashville, 1981).

7. Many of the 20 differences which Schaller lists in his book are only relevant to the US church culture. We have chosen seven which we believe are transferable to any small church, and are thus transcultural. The reader is directed to Appendix One where the complete list of Schaller's distinctions are listed.

8. See Carl S Dudley, 'Unique Dynamics of the Small Church', *Special Papers and Research Reports* (The Alban Institute Inc,: Washington, DC, 1977).

9. Dudley points out from the American context that small groups in the larger churches are more organised for specific purposes, such as prayer, study, events, interests, and causes. *Ibid* p 6. We might also note Paul Yonggi Cho's church in Korea as an example of a large mega-church which uses small groups effectively for growth and development. See his book *Successful Home Cell Groups* (Logos: 1981).

10. *Ibid* p 13. Dudley's discussion of the small church as a single-cell or primary group is worth examining.

11. See chapter 11.

12. Schaller suggests that the overwhelming majority of small-membership congregations on the North American con-

tinent are 'owned and operated' by the laity (*Ibid* p 28). He also notes that by contrast most of the decision making in larger churches is dominated by clergy.

13. Examples which come readily to mind are: who is able or allowed to preach; who can preside at the communion table (and if they 'do it right'); the minister as paid servant of the church and his 'rights'. Fortunately this scenario is being replaced in many sectors of the church.

14. Schaller, *Small Church is Different*, pp 28, 54.

15. Dudley, 'Unique Dynamics', p 18.

16. Schaller, *Small Church is Different*, p 29.

17. *Ibid*

18. See the discussion on the use of spiritual gifts in chapter 14.

19. See the article in *Alpha*, 'Can Small Be Beautiful?', by Catherine Butcher (July 1991), pp 34–36.

20. For example, Roy Pointer, 'How Do Churches Grow?' (as quoted in *Alpha*, p 35); Fred Smith, 'The Unique Role of the Smaller Church' in *Leadership* Vol 12, No. 4 (Fall 1991), pp 84–88.

21. One factor which all churches need to face is the important transition from the subsidy of the past to the reins of responsibility of the present and the future. This has serious consequences for the longevity of the church—especially in economic terms. Churches which are unwilling to spend funds which have been given in the past will find it hard to grow in faith for the future. Equally, churches which only live in the past cannot effect the needed impetus for strategies to face today and tomorrow. This vision element, which is needed, we will explore further in chapter 10.

PART 2
Issues For The Small Church

CHAPTER SIX

THE SMALL CHURCH PASTOR—A RARE BREED?

It was quickly becoming one of those weeks. The Sunday worship service was dull and flat, along with poor attendance. There were some unresolved tensions within our leadership which had not, as yet, been dealt with sufficiently. Some people who had promised to be available to do certain jobs had either forgotten (again) or ignored the need. The giving was down, enthusiasm was waning, problems were mounting, esteem had fallen. Again I asked myself—what on earth am I doing here with this group of 25 people?

I have been working as a minister of a small church for the past 10 years. Along with my theological training, I have worked with churches of 200, 400 and over 1000 people respectively, and began my current ministry with my family of 4 and 5 other adults. I have continued to read books on leadership, church growth, and mission. I have been fortunate to be a leader of ministers' fraternals and have valued friendships with many other leaders of small churches. Through all of this I have learned something very important. While most of the issues which face ministers/priests/pastors/leaders are similar in small, medium and large churches, there are some particular issues which are peculiar to those who are called to work in the smaller church. What are these unique problems?

I should state that there are two kinds of small churches where these may not apply. The first is the church which is still in its infancy after being planted and has not yet had time to develop and mature. The second is a small church which up until recently had been a medium or large church, but due to a period of turmoil has lost members due to unresolved conflicts, and has become smaller.

It is also true that all of the issues which will be highlighted in this chapter are related to the broader issues of conflict and risk-taking. These are part and parcel of the dynamics of leadership in the smaller church and cannot be overlooked or avoided.

Who Am I?

Self esteem

I have never met an honest church pastor who hasn't questioned his or her calling to leadership. This is especially true of those in the smaller church. When we first introduce ourselves to other church leaders, the usual questions are: Where do you come from; what is your denomination or affiliation, and what is the size of your church? This is why there is often a defensive response from the church leader of the smaller church (who is attempting to justify the apparent lack of success of his or her church). I have often heard this type of response spoken at conferences, at gatherings of ministers, in homes, over the phone, just about everywhere. Often it is spoken with a sense of failure, with strain and difficulty in the voice. The eyes and actions of the speaker conveying the sense of frustration and despondency.

God not only loves small churches, He also loves the small church pastor. I know that statement is not revolutionary, but it needs to be heard, believed and implemented in our lives. Our worth in God is not directly related to our success or failure in the work of the church. We need to feel our worth in God, as well as in our ministry and work for the Lord, whether we are working in a group of 5 or 5000.

The Old Testament gives us at least two clear examples of leaders who also were uncertain of their calling and needed their esteem to be elevated. In Exodus chapters 3 and 4 we see God calling Moses to lead His people. After the shock of the burning bush, Moses realises his inadequacy for such a task. He then begins to give many and various reasons why he is incapable of this work. He probably remembers his time in Pharaoh's court, his memory of the destruction at his hand of the Egyptian, and his consequent flight. He is both afraid of Pharaoh and of God. He is also afraid of failing in this important task.

A second example of a leader who equally felt uncertain is the prophet Jeremiah. Often in his writing we see him struggling with his calling and esteem from the opening chapters of the initial commission to be God's spokesperson, to his times of difficulty when there was a lack of response from the people to the word of God.

Both of these men struggled with their worth in God, with their calling and with their subsequent ministry. Moses was leading a large group, Jeremiah had few followers, even though he spoke to an entire nation. We, as small church leaders, often feel taken for granted, unrecognised for our hard work, effective ministry or loving care. We need to be reminded that this is part of the particular call of the pastor in the smaller church. We often don't receive the appropriate words of encouragement, or see the visible fruits of our labours as soon as we would like them. But, in the words of the late Francis Schaeffer, there are 'no little people' in the service of God.[1]

What Should I Do?

Time commitments

'Time' has become the four letter word of our generation. No one seems to know how best to use it. There never seems to be enough of it; managing it has become big business; especially for the busy and intense lives of today's Christian leaders, time has become an impossible companion in life.[2]

The pressures on time are the same in principle for all Christian leaders and workers, regardless of the number of people they are called to serve. The needs of time for God, for ministry, for family and friends, outside interests and for self can become a balancing act of great skill. But even in the area of time management, there are some peculiarities for the leadership of smaller churches.

Perhaps the most difficult conflict for the leader in a small church is the problem of managing time spent with the local church and time in other related areas of ministry. These can and often do include: a number of outside speaking or ministry engagements; educational pursuits; denominational commitments; parish or community responsibilities. The local congregation can easily be overlooked or even ignored for more illustrious and promising ministry somewhere else. I am not suggesting that there are not appropriate times for such ministry, or that some leaders are not especially gifted and called to this work. It is only a reminder of the need to find a balance of time for everything.

A small church with which I am familiar in the South East of England was at one time led by a full-time pastor and his family. After they had concluded their work and moved on, in the interim, the church called an American couple to work with them for a few months between placements. This American family had been used to working in some larger churches, and after adjusting to both culture shock and to the size of the church, they soon became frustrated because they did not feel that they had enough to do. After worship and preparation and visiting each member that week, they were at a loss to know where to begin. From their perspective, they could not imagine how anyone could work full-time in this kind of church situation. To be fair, they had not taken up residence in the community, so their expectations for themselves and the church were very different than for the previous and current minister (who is also full-time). But it does highlight the very real issue of how time is spent in the smaller church. (After all, I am writing this book and working in a small church).

I am not suggesting that leaders of smaller churches should not invest time and energy in other areas of ministry. However, impatience with the small church can cause that congregation to tear apart. The real question then becomes who is serving whom? The small church becomes nothing more than a stepping stone to a more lucrative position, or at least something which feeds the ego and needs of the minister for personal and work-related recognition.

It is my observation that when Christian leaders invest most of their energies in the smaller church, one of two things happens. Either the church begins to grow and eventually becomes a larger church, or their ministry is for a short duration of time and they move to new and greener pastures. The irony of this latter approach is that from all available research, the most productive years of the pastor's ministry come after years 4 to 6.[3] This is when the honeymoon period is over, the church begins to know the minister and trust his/her leadership. It is also the time when the leader begins to grasp the real issues facing the church and the community where it is located.

Personal time planning should become a priority for the pastor of the smaller church.[4] This becomes the framework for judging the allotment of time and the effectiveness of one's opportunities and diary. If I spend all my time visiting or counselling the flock, when will I have time for vision, planning for growth, development of new strategies in evangelism and leadership training, prayer and time to think? Equally if I spend all my available time in other avenues of service and ignore the church in my care, how can I say I am serving this church to which I have been called, as well as helping it to develop and grow?

When Will It Happen?

Self-expectations

Each time I attend a conference, read a book, or spend time with a Christian leader who is part of a large and growing church, I come away with mixed feelings. Often I am challenged, encouraged, and full of vision and possibilities. I am ready to change the world, and possibly the church! Other times I feel defeated, discouraged, and disappointed. I am ready to leave, I feel I am no good as a minister, and the church will never change. Perhaps I should stop attending conferences, reading books, and stay away from success stories of church growth!

I sense that when I am talking to many ministers who are serving in smaller churches there is a great deal of pressure on them to try to make the church succeed. 'I've got to make it grow' seems to be the battle cry of many dedicated, well trained men and women of God who are also frustrated. I don't think they are consciously trying to express unnecessary pathos. Rather they believe, they pray, they work, they expect miracles, and often all they see are the same few people week after week, with little or no change.

One important way of combatting this problem area is in the development of team ministry. Many church planting and evangelism initiatives which are currently being undertaken are using teams of people in their endeavours, and finding the work much more effective. This is also true of larger churches. The one-man band days are beginning to come to an end. But what of the smaller church? If I am working with only five or even 25 people, how do I as a leader think about and implement the idea of team?

I cannot stress enough the value of having a team of committed people to work beside me in the task of leading God's people. I do not have all the necessary gifts for leadership (even after 10 years of theological and Bible College training), so I need others who are gifted in areas where I am not, to share the load—both the work load and the people/emotions load of leadership.

It hardly needs pointing out that even Jesus had a team of three close followers, and the twelve, plus the women who often contributed financially, along with the wider network of disciples. This doesn't mean that there is not a need for a strong leader in the church. Even teams need leaders. But it does mean that one person doesn't have to carry the load of responsibilty alone. Learning to share leadership with others is one way of dealing with imbalanced self-expectations, along with helping one become accountable to a group of people who learn to know and trust you.

The obvious question which needs to be addressed is not do we need to work in teams, but where do these people who will form the teams come from? For some smaller churches, one model would be to form teams from outside the congregation, often for specific tasks. For example, in our church we do not have sufficient people to run a youth club. In order to meet this need, we have formed a team of workers from 4 different churches, who are working and being trained together. None of the churches could have an effective youth programme on their own. In addition, none of the churches had sufficient youth to make it work. But in working together, we have been able to help our young people to develop friendships and grow in their Christian faith, which would not have been possible on our own. (There is more on this in chapter 13).

A second model is the long-term view of leadership training with the intention of developing team leadership in the local church. The church I minister with has adopted this approach, and after 10 years of work, we are enjoying the fruit. It does mean asking God to show you the people who are both capable and willing to work in relationships with each other. It also means a costly commitment in time, training, and most importantly, trial and error. We have to create room for people to experiment and make mistakes with loving correction. Trust has to be developed, and this will not come overnight. There are no short term solutions in creating this model.

Finally, as a third example of developing team in the local church, the entire church body could act as a team. This already happens in many small churches of under 10 people. Each person has to play their part in keeping the church open and operative. Shared leadership could be divested as each person learns to take responsibility in various areas of work. Jesus' disciples were an example here. With only twelve in his team, Jesus invested in individuals to manage finance (even if it was Judas!), to work in teams for evangelism when the 12 and the 72 were sent out; to make preparations for the Passover; to investigate the resources available from the crowds of thousands to help feed them with loaves and fishes. Even though these are all tasks to be performed, they worked together to make Jesus' ministry more effective.

With all the talk and materials around today about the importance of team ministry and team work, I am still surprised at how often I find colleagues who either work alone because they cannot find anyone to work with them, or because they won't work with anyone else. Perhaps leaders need to make sure they are willing to invest in people and take some risks, and not continue to enlarge the clergy/laity divide.

There are other areas of a more deeply psychological nature in dealing with our self-expectations. Louis McBurney, in his book *Every Pastor Needs a Pastor*[5] has a number of helpful comments in this whole area, especially his concept of being called by God into freedom and fulfillment. There is no doubt that our own self-expectations play a significant role in the approach we have to our work in the small church, especially when we realise that we may not be 'where the action is'. We probably won't receive all the encouragement and support that we need from the church or our colleagues, but if we can learn to become content in our service with God, we might find our work more valuable and fulfilling.

Where Am I?

Length of ministry

While I was in college training for the ministry, I knew a man and his family who were working with a small church not far from the location of the school. He had spent about 3 or 4 years with the church while completing his degree. As the day of his graduation drew near, he made a very important decision. He would be willing to continue to work with this small church, which had no experience of long-term ministers, only students in training. He would help this church to address this need. Within one year, he soon realised that this church didn't really want to face such a challenge, and so he and his family left, leaving another training minister to take his place.

How long one stays in any given ministry is dependent on many issues. For some, the denomination has much to say about placement and length of service. For others, the church and minister work it out together in some way. The real issue is that the small church pastor is rarely seen by the church as staying long-term. Yet, as stated earlier, the best fruit in ministry for both minister and church comes after the 4–6 year warm-up period.

Someone once said 'the grass is always greener—but it still has to be cut!' If we are always looking over our shoulder at another prospective ministry, then we will miss the work of the Spirit in the place where we are. I can testify that after my first 6–7 years in a small church, there came a time of growth and blessing I would have missed had I not been there. And the growth continues to this day.

We need to allow the Lord to lead us into our futures, but we must be cautious in not overlooking what God is already doing in our church and community in the present.[6]

Why Should I?

Church and community expectations

Along with the self-expectations noted above, there are some very real and difficult tensions which small church pastors face in relation to the expectations that flow from the community where the church is situated.

It is important to discover what the stated, and unstated, expectations are in both the small church and in the community where the church is located. Often it can take time to discover what people mean by what they say. Statements about what the previous minister was like, or recollections of the good old days often help us understand what the 'hidden' expectations are, or at least what some think they should be.[7]

One of the most frequent comments I hear and read about is: 'That's what we pay you for, pastor!' The 'what' can be anything from visiting all the members, leading all the services, attending to all the meetings, even washing all the windows in the church. It seems to be a no win situation when a church expects the minister to be everything to everyone, a little less than God in working it all out, even more humble than Jesus, and poorer than anyone in all creation.

In addition to the expectation from the church, the community has its own unique set of expectations. I can remember my desire to get to know my community better. I decided the best way to do this was to become involved with the board of the local community residents association (no easy task!). I soon found myself deep in the problems and issues facing the community with a small band of people who were sure they knew what was best for the residents of the housing estate (often without asking them). I was the token religious representative, which gave me the unique privilege of judging the beauty contest, the dog show, and the garden produce. It was not part of my expectations when I joined, and though it provided the church with a couple of useful contacts, the involvement was short lived. It seemed that the community leaders and I had different expectations on what my work was about.

Expectations are not to be avoided, but they must be managed. As with the issues of time, we need to have clear goals and strategies which will force us to deal realistically with the demands and expectations of others with integrity and with our own giftedness and calling. As we share these with the church and the community, expectations should become clearer, and once expressed, should benefit our ministry.

How Can I?

Financial fears

There are only a handful of ministers who serve small churches who do not have some financial problems, worries, or difficulties. There is no question in my mind that many small churches do not contribute realistically to their ministers' wages and salaries. Most are subsidised in some way, either in denominational payments (although times are changing), or from the State.

I am writing as a pastor of a small church which is currently being subsidised. Most of my salary comes from another Christian source. This is in the process of change, and in the very near future, the church I serve will either have to go it alone and provide the full salary, or else I will have to consider part-time employment or moving. My wife is currently working outside the home to contribute as well. This scenario is not unusual in the small church.

Part of the issue that a small church and pastor need to work out is the question, 'is this job part-time or full-time?' Some ministry is only part time. Some is full-time, but needs some short-term subsidy. Other work is full-time and needs to be paid a full-time wage.

There are many quotes and humourous anecdotes concerning clergy and finance, but the realities are not usually funny. Financial issues cause much unnecessary stress to a minister and/or family who are attempting to be set apart to work for God in ways that others may not be able to. They should not be penalised for this.

One goal which the church and the pastor should agree to work towards is a plan of action to finance the ministry as soon as it is feasible and reasonable to do so. In this way, the minister can be released from unnecessary unstated expectations to work for nothing (and get it!) while attempting to do one's best for God.

One church I know has less than 50 members but has two full-time staff. They achieve this by regularly teaching on tithing, and expect all members to participate. Another church pays their minister a small wage, he and his family are given a car, plus expenses, and he receives income supplement for the remainder of the funds. Needless to say, the first minister has a better sense of value and appreciation, and probably this will be reflected in his ministry, even though both of them are serving the Lord well. A small church can effectively support a minister full-time if the job demands it, and if there are sufficient wage earners who will commit themselves to tithing or more in their giving.[8]

All the above mentioned items involve taking some risks for growth and development. They equally highlight some of the difficulties and issues which face the small church pastor. God has equipped the small church pastor with three qualities which not only help them to tackle these challenges, but also make small church leaders special men and women of God.

The Pastor is a Listener

Listening in ministry is always a three way exercise. First, there is the need to listen to God. Most medium and large church leaders find time for prayer and quiet very difficult in their busy schedules. The small church pastor often has the unique circumstances to be able to set some time aside to listen to God in prayer, in worship, and in reflection.

Secondly, listening is directed to the people. The face-to-face encounters found in the small church present the leader with the unique opportunity to actually listen to his people, to hear their stories of faith and growth (and failure) and to become a spiritual director (and there are not enough of these around).[9]

Thirdly, the listening ear is turned to the community. Again, the pastor is often in a unique position to relate to the people in his community in ways the pastor of a larger church is not. This is true not only in rural or inner city areas, but in many places, if he or she takes the time.

The tension in ministry is between leading and listening. In general, for the larger church leader, listening is undertaken primarily in order to lead more effectively. To hear what people, especially key people are saying, will influence the larger church's leadership and involvement in ministry. However, in the small church, listening is not just a means to improve ministry, it often constitutes ministry. Taking time to listen is one of the essential works of ministry in the small church. This is one of the strengths of the small church leader.

The Pastor is a Learner

Every pastor and leader is a learner. But as with the issues of listening, so also in learning, the goal is different for the larger and smaller church ministers. The larger church pastor primarily knows the programmes. He cannot possibly know each person intimately. He might not know the names, relationships, or work of each person in his church, but he does know the types of programmes that these people would most benefit from. The small church pastor knows his people, their names, their stories, their lives.

As in the description of the listener, the primary relationship here is with God. The small church pastor is usually not seen to be so professional that he forgets he also wears 'L' plates. He usually speaks of his own growth: victories and failures, strengths and weaknesses.

The pastor also seeks to learn about his flock. To know them is to love them. To walk with them in the good and bad, year after year, is to demonstrate something of the love of God in a unique way. The church knows their pastor cares if he or she takes time to learn about them and their lives.

The community is also an area of learning. Every community is unique with its own history, its own ethos, its own dynamic. Wise is the small church leader who learns his community and learns to minister as a member of it.

The Pastor is a Lover

For the pastor of a small church, this is the heart of the matter, being a lover. In the community, in the church, in his or her home, the love of God is demonstrated in the life and care of the minister. The one who loves God and his people is one who knows what ministry is all about.

Carl S. Dudley recognises that there are different ways of measuring the success and achievement of ministry. The small church has its own unique contribution to make. He comments:

> The pastor who feels a great need for constant and consistent measurement of achievement should not expect to find his or her calling to be satisfied by the strokes of a small congregation. But the pastor who finds reward in relationships with people—all sorts of people in all kinds of moods—should find love in the small church, and return love.[10]

Ian Bilby illustrates this principle very well. Ian is a New Zealander and Elim pastor who spoke in Birmingham to a group of Christian leaders from a variety of church backgrounds. He told this gathering the story of his very first ministry. In this small church of a few families, he was frequently frustrated, angry, and disappointed and was regularly tempted to depart for greener pastures. One day as he was moaning to God about the state of affairs of these people, God told him to learn to love and care for these sheep. He wrestled with this, but then determined that he would be the best lover of these sheep in his care as he was able. He learned that he was serving God first and then his people and that by becoming obedient to God with those in his care, God could then use him in other areas effectively. He had to first learn to get his priorities right, especially in the way he was using his time: from moaning to serving!

The small church pastor must remember that he is not just a leader who is over his people. He is one who is alongside his people, as one who serves in the day to day lives of his people, enabling them to know God, to trust Him, and to be led by Him.

Eugene Peterson echoes this when he states,

> The biblical fact is that there are no successful churches. There are, instead, communities of sinners, gathered before God week after week in towns and villages all over the world. The Holy Spirit gathers them and does his work in them. In these communities of sinners, one of the sinners is called *Pastor* and given a designated responsibility in the community. The pastor's responsibility is to keep the community attentive to God.[11]

This, then, is the heart of leadership ministry in the small church. The pastor who can emulate the expressions of listening, learning, and loving will incarnate the servant-leadership style of Jesus to his congregation. And he or she may very well find love and acceptance in return.

Notes

1. Francis Schaeffer. *No Little People. Sixteen Sermons for the 20th Century* (Intervarsity Press: Downers Grove, 1974), pp 13–25.
2. On time management in general, see Ted Engstrom and Alex MacKenzie *Managing Your Time* (Zondervan: Grand Rapids, 1968); and David Cormack *Seconds Away* (Marc Europe: London, 1986).

3. See the information in C Peter Wagner, *Leading Your Church to Growth* (Marc: London, 1984), pp 69–70, 103. See also Paul Beasley-Murray and Alan Wilkinson *Turning the Tide* (Bible Society: London, 1981), p 34. Wagner in his work quotes Lyle Schaller *Assimilating New Members* (Abingdon Press: Nashville, 1978), for further elucidation on this point.

4. The issues of goal setting is, in my view primary for the small church leader. In addition to the comments found in Chapter 12 of this book, the reader can also benefit from reading the following works: Edward R Dayton and Ted W Engstrom, *Strategy for Leadership* (Marc: London, 1985 ed), Chapter 5: 'The Awesome Power of Goals' pp 51–68; C Peter Wagner, *Leading Your Church to Growth*, pp 186–190; Roy Pointer, *How Do Churches Grow?* (Marshalls: Basingstoke, 1984), pp 142–172; and most recently Peter Brierley *Priorities, Planning and Paperwork* (Monarch: Tunbridge Wells, 1992), pp 17–42.

5. Louis McBurney, *Every Pastor Needs a Pastor* (Word Books: Waco, 1977).

   Especially helpful are part one: 'The Call: Invited or Inducted?', pp 17–36, and part two: 'The Encumbered' pp 37–56, which deals primarily with expectations most ministers feel and how to learn to relax and deal with them.

   He has also written, with David McCasland, a further condensed article on the issues of roles and expectations in 'The Danger of Aiming Too High' in *Leadership* Vol 5, No. 3 (Summer 1984): pp 30–35.

6. A helpful article for someone either new into the small church or feeling they are getting nowhere is David Hansen, 'Upon Taking a Small Church', in *Leadership* Vol 11, No. 2, pp 78–79. Also see John H Atkinson, 'The Country Chapel: is small really beautiful?' in *The Circuits*, pp 8–10, who gives some encouragement from the Methodist perspective.

7. See Richard P Hansen 'The Sound of Clashing Expectations', In *Leadership* Vol 5, No. 3 (Summer 1984): pp 78–83.

8. For a fuller treatment of this issue, see the discussion on finance in Chapter eight.

9. Eugene Peterson calls the work of a spiritual director as '. . . giving attention to what God is doing in the person who happens to be before me at any given moment.' *Working the Angles*: *The Shape of Pastoral Integrity* (Eerdmans Publishing Co: Grand Rapids, 1987), p 2; also pp 103–131. His earlier article 'The Unbusy Pastor' in *Leadership* Vol 2, No. 3 (Summer 1981): pp 70–77, has much to commend in the areas of listening and spiritual leadership.

10. Carl S Dudley *Making the Small Church Effective* (Abingdon: Nashville, 1978), pp 73–74.

11. Eugene Peterson *Working the Angles*, p 2.

CHAPTER SEVEN

LEADING THE SMALL CHURCH

In his recent book *Dynamic Leadership*,[1] Paul Beasley-Murray begins by calling for more leaders for churches. What he means is not just more numbers of leaders (although some denominations do have such a significant need) but rather the right calibre and type of leaders.

Even with the flood of books and materials in the Christian market on leadership,[2] very few really address the particular needs and approaches of leading the smaller church. This does not invalidate these contributions. Their expertise and wisdom have proven helpful to many leaders of all sizes of church. The problem is that just as the small church is not a smaller version of a larger church, so leadership within it is also unique and needs to be addressed with this in mind.

There are two specific areas within which leadership is unique for the smaller church. Without an adequate grasp of these, a church leader will soon become disillusioned, discouraged, and ineffective in his or her leading of the church.

Resistance to Leadership

Much, if not most, leadership in the small church is in fact resisted. There are a variety of reasons for this seemingly illogical approach.

One reason is that the minister is seen to be 'outside', hence not one of us. Whether in the form of language, culture, social status, or even just because of his or her training, the pastor is often treated as an alien in a foreign land. So there will be both a resistance and a reluctance from the congregation to accept the minister because of this perception. Some clergy have found this to be true, or at least felt it was a genuine response from their congregation. Class distinctions, though less of a problem than in days of old, are still relevant to styles and approaches to ministry. Those from rural settings find inner city ministry uninviting, and those who were raised in the commuter belt find small towns a struggle.

Carl S. Dudley reminds us of the tension this creates for both pastor and church:

> The clergyperson is often born elsewhere, has a uniquely different education, depends upon regional denominational leadership for recognition and advancement, and personally maintains a system of values not completely in harmony with those of the congregation.[3]

A second reason for this resistance is the area of tradition and history. Every church is a carrier of its past memories and traditions. I like to think of this as 'holy history'. Significant events, key people, shared experiences, all combine to evoke the collective memory of each church and each member. For some, conversations will focus on the good old days, for others there may be pain or heartache. Some will focus on a memorable leader, others will recall a special event or service. All of it is part of the rich tapestry of the life of this church.

Trained clergy have no immediate access to this treasure house of the small church. It would take time to learn about it. Since most clergy in small churches don't stay for a long pastorate, they never become part of this historical process. They cannot gain access because they know (and the members know) that they will soon be off to new pastures. So it is never learned, and consequently ignored. Many others do not want to recognise the past. They are wanting to move forward, not look back. So it is subsequently set aside or even rejected outright.[4]

This makes the small church feel insignificant, as if all that has gone on before is trivial. They have worked together, prayed together, worshipped together, built memories of faith and trust. Now this is being set aside. Hence, resistance is expressed towards the leadership.

A third reason for resistance has to do with power. Effective leadership in the small church is not primarily 'from above' but 'alongside'. This is due to the fact that in the smaller church, motivation and response is based much more on relationships with people than on structured programming. Larger churches operate on a highly-structured management model for the clergy. This is essential for the church to operate efficiently and effectively. Smaller churches express a different modus operandi, expressed in two ways.

First, the laity are significant to the life of the church. They are not just there to supply workers to accomplish tasks. They actually provide the leadership. They are often better informed of the small church network of relationships than the clergy, they have lived in the community longer, they have been a part of this family and know and cherish many of its traditions. They are the leaders. As Lyle Schaller observes:

> In the large congregation, most of the members expect the minister to be the leader, but in the small congregations the members expect the pastor will be one of several leaders, and not necessarily the most influential member of that leadership team.[5]

Secondly, the members often express the feeling that 'we don't want to be told what to do.' By this they are not suggesting that new input is unwelcome. Rather, they are indicating that receiving orders from on high and carrying them out is not the way of the small church. Steve Burt, in his excellent book on small church leadership, reminds us that members of small churches want to be motivated to make their decisions. He writes:

> Small churches need good small church pastors, women and men who can provide leadership rather than management, who can build up the laity and inspire them so they trust themselves to make decisions and follow through rather than to simply hear decisions and carry out orders.[6]

Leadership indicates power. The small church has its own form of power. Therefore to become an effective leader in the small church, the minister must begin to realise that the small church wants someone not to stand over them, but to stand beside them.[7]

Leadership Development

The question many ministers ask is, 'How do we find, encourage, nurture and develop leaders in the small church'. If you are faced with a congregation of 10 elderly parishoners, or 20 middle-aged families who began church work 10 years ago, where will new leadership come from? This is a significant question. Small churches essentially rely on volunteers who often get worked until they burn out. For the church to grow, there is a need to develop new programmes, and there simply isn't the staff or resources to move ahead. This is a great source of frustration for all small church leaders.

A study by the Baptist Union entitled *Half the Denomination* (those congregations having 50 or less people), expressed the importance of leadership development in small churches like this:

> Many small churches regard 'lack of leadership' as the largest obstacle to their progress. The lack is often expressed in terms of people: there is no-one to teach in Sunday School, run the youth group, or officer the church. Sometimes the lack is just one person: someone who can give co-ordination and direction to the whole life of the Christian community. There is no-one who can bring new ideas and motivate the people for service and mission.[8]

It further states:

> A leadership is required which can recognise and develop these primary potential strengths of personal relationships, with uncluttered concentration on worship and lay participation.[9]

John Finney, the Church of England Officer for the Decade of Evangelism until his recent appointment as a bishop, suggests in his recent book on leadership and mission, that one priority of leadership is to '. . . see the discovery, training, and use of other leaders as one of their main tasks.'[10]

But recognising the need and finding the people are often poles apart in the smaller church. Even though there are no short-term solutions to this genuine dilemma, one essential response is in the development of giftedness within the members of the church. Some suggestions as to how leaders can learn to accomplish this can be found in Chapter fourteen.

We have already mentioned in the previous chapter that the qualities needed for ministering with the small church focus on the role of the pastor as a lover, more than the particular style or type of leadership expressed. Just as the life of the congregation is primarily relational, so is leadership in a small church.[11]

But what does such a leader look like? Steve Burt gives the following job description of what every small church is looking for in their pastor:

> The results of a computerised survey indicate that the perfect small church pastor preaches exactly fifteen minutes, condemning sin but never upsetting anyone. He works from 8am until midnight, makes thirty pounds a week, wears smart attire, buys good books, drives a good car, and gives about thirty pounds a week to the poor. The perfect small church pastor is twenty-eight years old and has been preaching for twenty-five years. He has a burning desire to work with teenagers and loves to spend all his time with OAP's. The perfect small church pastor makes fifteen visits daily on parish families, the housebound and those in hospital. He spends all his time evangelising the unchurched, and is always available in his study when needed.[12]

How Do I Love Thee?

In the previous chapter, we considered the role of the pastor, and in particular the qualities which would make them most effective. The final quality mentioned was recognising that the pastor in the small church is essentially a lover. Because small churches resist leadership, motivational leadership is crucial. Regardless of how many men and women may be queuing up to fulfill the post of the small church pastor, the reality is that because of its relational nature, the small church is crying out for a leader who is primarily a lover. We then need to ask: How does a lover lead?

A Lover leads by listening

Ask any minister or counsellor to list one of the major difficulties faced by married couples and the reply will inevitably be lack of communication. A Cliff Richard song illustrated this when he sang 'We don't talk anymore.' Perhaps the reality is that too many are talking and not enough are listening. By learning to listen, we will discover the person we are caring for and learn to love them more deeply. This is vital in our ministry in the small church.

Listening involves time, spending time with each person, demonstrating that they are important to God, that their life matters to the Kingdom. In a world where everything is constantly changing, and the individual is often ignored or overlooked for the sake of the group, a small church pastor who offers to listen to people will reap a harvest of insights into the fabric of the church and community where he serves.

We have already mentioned the value of history, but this can only be gathered and learned by listening. For many small churches, the talk may be of older and better days, when the church was full, or just in its infancy. These stories are part of the everyday life of the congregation, and need to be heard and expressed. Listening is a powerful way of demonstrating our love for our people—it helps them to feel valued. 'In an anonymous world, the small church calls us by name'.[13] We are indeed important to God.

A lover leads by involvement

Many of the studies on leadership come out of management theory and practice. These can be very helpful, but ask anyone who has worked on the shop floor, and you will be told in so many words what the workers think of management. There is a distinct dislike because 'they don't care'. By its very nature, management is removed from the worker. It is the case of being 'over' the ones who are 'under'. This pyramid viewpoint can also be found in many places, including some churches.

The problem for the small church is twofold. The pastor, as we mentioned above, is usually an outsider, coming from another place (culturally, ethnically, sociologically, often academically). He is also endued with some sort of authority, and so often gives an account outside the church to other leaders. The friendships and support for the pastor are also found primarily outside the local church. All of this causes a sense of alienation between the minister and the congregation.

The second problem is one of time. The members have often been around for many years, and know that this minister will only be here for a limited period of time. They, along with the church's work, will still remain long after the minister moves on, often to better and greener pastures.

These are hard realities which must be faced. But a lover can help overcome some of this tension by changing the perception from 'over' 'under' and 'outside' to 'with them' or 'beside them'. This is the model of the incarnation which God demonstrated in Jesus when he came from glory to become a man and identify with his people in a specific way (as Paul celebrates in the hymn in Philippians 2:5–11). Even after Jesus left, the Holy Spirit was sent to be our advocate—to come alongside us and be with us always.

A pastor who can follow Jesus in this way, by participating as one of the people of God, by involvement in the daily events of people's lives, no matter how small or insignificant, by 'touch' and by friendship, will be very effective in leading his small church. Jesus was the friend of sinners, and as leaders we also must learn to befriend our people, to walk with them through the joys and sorrows of life, to come along beside them.

A lover leads by example

'Follow my example as I follow the example of Christ Jesus.' So says Paul the apostle to the Christians in Corinth. Most pastors and leaders would also like to echo these words of Paul. Many fine examples of Christian leadership are to be found among the small church pastors throughout this country. They will never write a book, speak at a conference, receive the recognition other named Christian leaders will have, but they are leading their churches by following their Lord Jesus. And there is a real power in their example.[14]

Ted Engstrom reinforces leadership by example when he states:

> Jesus' kind of service sets an example. He was willing to wash his disciples' feet. His perfect, sinless, human life ended in self-sacrifice at Calvary. Thus He showed His followers how to serve, and He demanded no less of those who would carry on His work on earth.[15]

Unfortunately, not everything we do is always noteworthy, but it is surely to be recognised and remembered by our churches. As an example, I can still recall a certain baptismal service which didn't quite go as expected. We had been using another church for our baptisms, and since we practice total immersion of adults, I had acquired a pair of fishing waders to keep my trousers dry. These worked well in the baptistry of the church that we visited. But when we relocated the services to a friend's swimming pool, I had not allowed for the difference in depth. The pool was much deeper, and after descending the stairs into the pool, I soon realised that the waders were going to be too small. I pressed on ahead and as the first wader submerged into the water, a loud rushing sound resembling a noisy kiss filled the air, first with one then the other wader. This caused much laughter and fun—at my expense. But there was more to come, after the baptism, as I was leaving the pool. The waders were obviously filled with water, and as I ascended out onto the steps, there was a distinctive 'slush' sound which followed me around the rest of the day. I would like to forget this, but my small church congregation enjoy reminding me regularly.

Whether our remembered example is one of demonstrating great faith or providing great fun, a small church will look to us in being an example of being 'real'.[16]

A lover leads by serving

It is precisely here that genuine ministry is separated from just doing a job. Jesus was willing to become a living parable of Kingdom values when he washed the feet of his disciples (Jn 13:1–17). He not only set them an example, but demonstrated what leadership in Kingdom terms was all about. His words stand in contrast to the disciples who wished to argue about the best seat in the throneroom, demonstrating that Jesus came not to be served but to serve. (Mark 10:45) This is the way of all true ministry.

The small church pastor is in a unique position to impact the members of his church in a way that leaders of larger churches can never achieve. Bearing in mind that Jesus invested most of his time in the lives of the 12 and especially the 3 close disciples, a small church leader must learn to serve his people in love.

Most of the work of a servant is not exciting. Setting out chairs, washing up after a church tea, taking someone home who is out of our way of travel, these and many other avenues of service have been part of my experience of the small church. They are not always stimulating, they receive little recognition, but they are at the heart of all authentic ministry, and the small church can only be effectively led by one who is willing to serve the Lord in their church and community.

Again, as Ted Engstrom suggests,

'Jesus teaches all leaders for all time that greatness is not found in rank or position but in service. He makes it clear that true leadership is grounded in love which must issue in service.'[17]

A lover leads by loving

One way to see what kind of leader you are is to see who is following you. Perhaps this is why the use of the shepherd as a model for leadership is so pronounced in Scripture. The Palestinian shepherd, unlike his Western cousin, leads his flock out of love.

John Stott, in his recent book *The Contemporary Christian*, suggests that we undershepherds learn to understudy Jesus, our Great Shepherd. He identifies seven key characteristics which are part of the shepherds work. Thus the shepherd:

1) knows his sheep (by name);
2) serves his sheep;
3) leads his sheep;
4) feeds his sheep;
5) rules his sheep;

6) guards his sheep;
7) seeks his sheep.[18]

This list of the characteristics of the shepherd of Palestine is also the pattern of Jesus' ministry. As our Great Shepherd, his ministry is the prototype of ours. He has established the pattern of servant leadership, of shepherding and loving us, and we must follow his example of leading as a lover. By leading and serving in this way, we shall begin to build trust and confidence between our people and ourselves. This in turn will enhance the recognised authority imparted to us by the congregation.

A story is told in an issue of *Leadership* of a small church which had to give an annual report to their denomination on the work of their minister. The leader was not allowed in the discussions. Afterwards, one of the leaders came to the minister and asked if he wanted to see what they had written. He was handed a small piece of paper which said 'We love our pastor and our pastor loves us.'

Can anything better be said of us in our ministry than we love and are loved? There is no better place to demonstate and experience this than in the smaller church.

NOTES

1. Paul Beasley-Murray, *Dynamic Leadership: rising above the chaos of the one-man band*, (Marc: Eastbourne, 1990).
2. Among the many helpful books on leadership not mentioned elsewhere in this chapter, the following have proven valuable: John Finney, *Understanding Leadership*, (Darton, Longman and Todd: London, 1989); J Oswald Sanders, *Spiritual Leadership* (Marshall Morgan and Scott: London, 1967); Eddie Gibbs, *Followed or Pushed*? (Marc: Bromley, 1987); Eddie Gibbs, *I Believe in Church Growth*, revised edition (Hodder and Stoughton: London, 1984); and Tom Marshall, *Understanding Leadership* (Sovereign World Ltd: Chichester, 1991).
3. Carl S Dudley, *Making the Small Church Effective* (Abingdon: Nashville, 1978), p 63.

4. A fuller discussion can be found in Chapter six.
5. Lyle Schaller, *The Small Church is Different!* (Abingdon: Nashville, 1982), p 44.
6. Steve Burt, *Activating Leadership in the Small Church: Clergy and Laity Working Together* (Judson Press: Valley Forge, 1988), p 25.
7. *Ibid* p 26.
8. *Half the Denomination*: The report of the working group on the care of small churches (The Department of Ministry/ Baptist Church House: London, 1983), pp 22–23.
9. *Ibid* p 11.
10. John Finney, *Church on the Move: Leadership for Mission* (Darton, Longman and Todd: London, 1992), p 10.
11. This is the conclusion of both Carl S. Dudley, *Making the Small Church Effective* (Abingdon: Nashville, 1978), p 72, as well as Lyle Schaller, *The Small Church is Different* (Abingdon: Nashville, 1982), pp 25–26.
12. Steve Burt, *Activating Leadership in the Small Church*, p 91. I have anglicized this for an English audience.
13. On the cover of *Making the Small Church Effective* by Carl S. Dudley.
14. See the helpful comments on the power of personal example and integrity by David Cohen and Stephen Gaukroger, *How to Close Your Church in a Decade* (Scripture Union: London, 1992), pp 45–49.
15. Ted Engstrom, *The Making of a Christian Leader* (Zondervan: Grand Rapids, 1976), p 37.
16. Steve Burt, *Activating Leadership in the Small Church*, pp 27–34.
17. Ted Engstrom, *The Making of a Christian Leader*, p 37.
18. John Stott, *The Contemporary Christian* (InterVarsity Press: Leicester, 1992), pp 279–290. His discussion of each of these characteristics is worth reading and pondering.

CHAPTER EIGHT

FINANCING THE SMALL CHURCH

Not many years ago, a survey was carried out among unchurched
people in America to ask them about their impressions of the
church. The results were varied, but one essential problem
continued to be highlighted. One difficulty which the respondents
had with the church was that church people '. . . are always
sad, or they talk about death, or they ask for money.'[1]

I have heard this same attitude towards the church and
money expressed by unchurched people in Britain. One such
comment was that 'The church always seems to be begging for
more money.' Perhaps this is a reflection on the tremendous
number of jumble sales, fêtes, coffee mornings, and appeals for
building funds which are held by various churches throughout
the course of each year all over the country. Whatever the
reason, there seems to be a definite negative impression being
given by the church that money is needed, wanted, and soon.
Unfortunately, this attitude is not exclusive to the unchurched.
It is my observation that it can also be found among Christians.

Attitudes to Giving

Attitudes to money, and especially to Christian giving, can be
summarised into three broad categories. First, the cultural
mentality of the unchurched who occasionally enter the doors
of the church. There is a general belief that the clergy/minister
is somehow paid for by the government. Perhaps this is a
reflection on the State church status of the Anglicans. Therefore

whenever money is asked for, there is strong resistance to giving, and the observation that all the church ever asks for is money. In addition to this, the way the church has used its money will also generally reflect on the unchurched attenders attitude. Some recent American models of not asking for money from the unchurched is one attempt to address this important issue.[2]

Secondly, the attitude of the Free Churches in general assumes a 'private club' mentality whereby Christian giving in practical terms is associated with a subscription fee. The denomination may suggest an amount from each church to be contributed. Some of this money goes to a central fund to help the denomination run effectively. This can been seen by the members as 'paying our dues' to the organising body, thereby reinforcing this observation and feeling.

One of my friends expressed this problem to me at a conference we were attending. His particular denomination had required that certain percentages of the offerings were sent to fund various activities and committees which were set up by the central body of the denomination. He and his church felt frustrated that so much of their giving was directed in this way. They would have prefered to be autonomous enough to decide how all the monies were used.

The final attitude is that of the small church. Here we are entering a new world of understanding. In general terms, the small church does not operate on a budget system in quite the way that a larger church does. Giving is not expressed in an objective statement of need, like that found in budget statements. Instead, giving is related to felt need. It has to be personalised. This causes obvious frustrations for both clergy and denominations. The ministers are often trained to work with the facts and figures of a budget. Quite often the denomination expects churches to operate in this same way. This is an apparent weakness for the small church. The subsequent giving cannot effectively be monitored, the church is unclear whether it is on course for reaching the needed funding, the programming will ultimately be affected and possibly hindered.

But the small church has its own way of coping and surviving, and this creates its strengths. Small churches have ways of inducing participation in its giving. Personal needs, missionaries known to certain members, particular projects, all seem to find the needed funding, whether a budget suggests this is possible or not. This then gives way to a variety of responses to meet the needs of the church. Various fund raising events, such as jumble sales, bric-a-brac, fêtes, and special appeals, often for building needs, are some of the usual expressions of response to needed funding. In addition, small churches are run on various forms of subsidy, and quite often on money provided from the denomination. Each of these expresses a part of the response which is made by the members of the small church to the needed funds for running the church.

Christian Giving in the Smaller Churches

The giving was far behind the budget, and the rent for the community centre we use for our church was behind more than one month. Each week on the notice sheet the budget needs are clearly printed with a weekly and monthly category along with the previous week's collection. But the deficit was mounting. Action could have been taken and either we would have to look for another place to worship, or not pay my salary. Once the figure of needed finance was mentioned, along with the impending crisis, the offering covered all but £20 of the total amount, which was subsequently met. This was obviously God's provision, but it also serves to illustrate one way in which small churches operate.

Giving is to a perceived need.

This cannot be overstated or overlooked if we are to understand and learn to minister effectively within the small church network. As Lyle Schaller has pointed out:

> One reason why small-membership congregations are so tough . . .
> is that the members do rally around and respond to a clear and
> visible need. . . . the dependability of the people in responding in
> a time of need is one of the distinctive characteristics of the small
> congregation.[3]

That need will often be a crisis situation. More often than not, the crisis will cause the church members to reach into otherwise empty pockets and pull out the magical rabbit with just enough money in his mouth to provide for what is needed.

This primary approach reflects the *psychological* meaning of giving for the congregation. A corporate catharsis is expressed by alleviating the impending trauma through giving to meet the need. The feeling of relief (whether expressed vocally or not) is released by the congregation as another seemingly formidable crisis is alleviated for the moment.

Giving reinforces community.

It actually is part of the glue that holds the family of God together. Everyone joins in meeting the need, and believes that the current situation is nothing new. The Lord has provided in the past, and He will somehow provide again. The people have responded in the past, and they will somehow respond again.

Perhaps part of the reason why the smaller church finds it so difficult to operate in a business approach (with budget, financial figures, goals) is that the framework is too detached. The felt or real needs of the smaller church are in the forefront, revealed in a reactive approach to giving. In a larger church, which adopts the business approach, the giving is essentially proactive. The sense of community or family is less crucial in the larger church, especially with regard to giving. But in the small church, being a family is what it is all about.

This second approach reflects the *social* meaning of giving. The ways and means of giving are just as important as any amount which is raised. This is one reason why much giving in the small church is expressed in a social setting. The use of jumble sales, fêtes, and fund-raising events are part of this overall spectrum. The events give full expression to the response of the congregation. Not only are they attempting to deal with the needed finance, but they are creating a social network of relationships which reinforces the caring nature of the church.

Even though my church attempted to operate on a business model, with budget, financial figures printed weekly, and goals, not until the finances became a felt need, did the church respond in a corporate fashion to meet this invading crisis (look what's happening to our church), and the needed money was forthcoming. Then the crisis was alleviated temporarily, and we could again resume our sense of belonging to each other and to a God who loves and provides our every need.

Giving directly involves each person.

Everyone's contribution, no matter how large or small is valued and praised. Not every member gives in a responsible or sacrificial manner. Some give a very small and insubstantial amount in comparison to the needs. This is partly reflected in the earlier comments about paying a subscription. In the Free Churches this attitude is paralleled in the social clubs of the local community. To be a member, you pay an annual fee. And this same mindset, which is often not conscious, can be found in the general giving of many small church members.

This final approach reflects the *personal* meaning of giving. I give because I am valued, I am loved, I am part of this community of believers. And my contribution is valued not so much for the amount as for the expression of giving in the life of this church. The focus is not pound signs but participation.

One church just outside of Nottingham was faced with the challenge to provide some of the support needed to fund a missionary to Africa. One young woman in the congregation took it upon herself to use a variety of projects, such as coffee mornings, car washes, and sponsored events, to raise a substantial amount of the capital fund needed. The church through its budget would never have given such a significant amount. This individual, however, knew the missionary and chose to use whatever means were available to make a rather large and needed contribution. The giving in this context was personal.

An inner city congregation were struggling to meet their needs. The minister's salary was behind, the roof needed repairing, and there had been some recent internal conflict, so there were less members to actually give to the church. Their response was to have a special gift day. Each person was encouraged to pray and respond in a generous way to meet the needs of 'our church and our minister.' Needless to say, the gift day was quite successful, and that little church was able to make a big difference to their overall finances. Each member had a personal interest in the continuation of the church and their minister, whom they loved. This prompted their response to the potential crisis. Their giving was personal.

Describing how the small church expresses its giving illustrates the need to understand its uniqueness. It does not easily operate in the world of budgets with regard to its finance. This is too cold and not felt personally. However, there are some strategies which will help the small church become more effective in its giving.

Strategies for Giving in the Smaller Church

Recognise and accept subsidy as a reality

There are no known churches which have never been subsidised at some point in time. Whether with prayer, time, work, dreams, vision, and of course money, most churches could not be where they are today without the generosity and grace of other Christian believers. Many small churches began life as frontier congregations building with just a limited amount of resources. Many small churches continue in this approach of sharing resources for their own life and witness.

The issue facing the small church is not whether it should be subsidised so much, as whether it is able to recognise the reality of the subsidy that continues to operate. Such honesty is important in understanding whether the particular subsidy is helpful or harmful. Is the subsidy creative and does it release growth and potential in the local church and its members? Or is it in fact debilitating, creating an impossible scenario in which the small church cannot see past the tug of the financial chord, which often includes certain expectations and in the worst cases, manipulation.

The small church I serve has been subsidised for the past 10 years. Most of this subsidy consisted in providing my salary. But changes are underway for the church to take up more responsibility for itself. The church is learning to give sacrificially in order to pay part of my salary. This has been a needed transition, but there have been struggles. Anthony Pappas, in his important book on the subject of financing the small church indicates that the struggle is valuable and needed in the life of the church. He comments:

> Life is struggle . . . the rule is blood, sweat, and tears, sacrifice and work, vision and hope . . . the rule is toughing out the lean years, keeping the doors open so that when the Spirit of God chooses to move there will be at least a point of beginning. Life in the small church is struggle. A struggle of faith. A struggle of fellowship. A struggle of fidelity. Thus it is . . . in the small church, life is struggle. But struggle is also life. . . Somehow God gives the power to remain steadfast in the struggle. And more than this—God uses our struggles as a means of growth for us.[4]

Some subsidy is not very desirable. One example is the situation where a minister must be subsidised out of private funds. I have more than one friend ministering in small churches who previously trained in another field of employment. They have built up a sizeable nest egg, which is now regularly drawn from to top up the salary in order to be financially viable.

Another option, which I encounter rather too frequently, is a church which relies heavily on the State to provide much of the income and housing for their minister. He or she is considered unemployed and on the dole, but the church pays some of their expenses. A related type of subsidy is where the salary is so small, that there is heavy reliance on income supplement to a very large measure. In the last two examples, the subsidy (primarily from the State) is very debilitating, often when compared with other local ministers of similar churches.

Small churches will often accept subsidy until they are forced to face its withdrawal. Facing such an issue might well seem cruel, but the alternatives might be worse.

Direct giving to projects not programmes

I have tried to suggest and illustrate that in the smaller church, giving which is directed to projects will produce the required amounts more quickly than will programmes which are part of the budget. This is due to the personal nature commented on above. A programme is impersonal and cold. It is something 'out there', like an alien from another planet. But *our* minister, *our* need for a new heating system (because we are freezing), *our* missionary, these are seen and felt as personal. They are close and within our reach.

One of the largest parts of a small church budget is the salary of the minister. Members of small churches might have to face the struggle of either buying themselves a new car, or continuing to provide (or learning to provide) their minister's salary. I can still recall the heartfelt gratitude of my first minister as he told how God continued to meet the needs of his family through the sacrifices of the members of his small church. There were days when gratitude was expressed for having enough money for a loaf of bread. But the church continued to be faithful in its giving, so 'our minister' was looked after.

The larger church has a difficult time understanding this, as do some small churches. In particular, this situation often requires the giving of a variety of people outside the fellowship of the church. This can create a difficult tension. Schaller comments that this struggle must be resolved, and offers six models for attempting to do so.[5] Whatever is decided, this strategy helps to segment the total needs into manageable chunks which then are responded to in a personal way.

Interdependence not independence

We do well to remind ourselves that the issues of subsidy also finds expression in the life of New Testament congregations. 2 Corinthians chapters 8 and 9 offer much reflection on the sharing of resources, including the giving of money between congregations in need as part of the larger body of Christ.

A debilitating use of subsidy will create dependence. I am not aware of any church which would welcome this as a regular approach. Many churches wish for independence. The whole area of paying for one's own minister is often the goal of each church, and needs to be examined carefully. Many small churches, perhaps even the majority, have clergy which are subsidised in a variety of ways. Whether through denomina-tional backing for a full-time post, or a combination of two salaries (part-time with a second job, or spouses' income added), or the increasing example of a part-time ministry with a full time job. It is not the normal pattern for a small church to have a full-time minister entirely paid for by that congregation, but it can be a goal to work towards.[6]

We must learn to recognise the value of interdependence. Where small churches begin to share resources with each other they will become more effective in their life and work. Chapter 13 offers some suggestions as to ways this might be accomplished.

One model of this is in the multi-church parish, where the minister's time is shared between two or more churches (here the Methodists have a very long track record). This creates certain advantages for smaller churches. It allows one staff member to work part-time (often there is not genuine full-time work for the smaller church), while doing the same with one or more other churches in a given area. Staff and their available time (which obviously needs to be worked out between the cooperating churches) is shared along with the financial load, especially where there is little or no denominational input.

Another potential model is in the use of students who are training. These students are members of their home churches, but have left to prepare themselves for the ministry. These men and women have certain limitations as to their availability due to their studies, but can find the opportunities to learn with a body of believers to be rewarding for them in training, as well as the church learning to love someone who is just beginning. They are being shared between their home church and the church where their practical training is taking place.

In my training days, this model was fairly common. Many of the smaller churches which were quite accessible to the college were staffed by students. They would be able to give 2–5 years of ministry, while being supervised by local leaders as well as tutors. This gave them hands-on experience, an opportunity to make mistakes (which I beleive is vital), as well as offering small congregations an opportunity to have ministry at a minimal cost.

A third option is where two or more congregations work together on a specific project which affects their life and growth. Our local churches are involved in a church planting project which is seeking to combine the resources and strengths of three small church congregations with the staffing of a recent graduate from training college. Each of the churches would be hard pressed to make any significant contribution on their own. The family who will be initiating the work would not have the necessary resources in people, finance, and prayer from any single congregation. But by cooperating in an interdependence model, each congregation can participate at the level where they can be most effective, and the family can receive the needed support to get the new work off the ground.

This also suggests a very important tension for the small church. How can a church which is being financially subsidised give something back? The three churches in the immediate example above are all currently being subsidised. Yet they are all involved in a cooperative venture of faith with a new church work, and are learning to demonstrate that small churches must learn to give as well as receive.

Interdependence is a good New Testament model to resurrect for the many small churches throughout the country. It has drawbacks and potential dangers of which the cautious reader will no doubt be aware. But when we consider that this practice was not uncommon in the early church, it has much to commend itself to us today.[7]

Motivating for mission rather than maintenance

The only direct statement of Jesus found outside the Gospels is expressed on the lips of the Apostle Paul in his farewell address to the Ephesians. In Acts 20:35, he informs the listeners that their ministry, which was funded at the work of their own hands, enabled them to assist in meeting the needs of the poor. This is related to the words of Jesus, 'It is more blessed to give than to receive.'

Even small churches need to learn to participte in the privilege and responsibility of engaging in mission outside themselves.[8] A very important strategy for Christian giving is to encourage the church to become actively involved in works of mission. Whether this is in supporting a foreign missionary, in aiding a church in the second, third, or fourth world, or even in having a special appeal for a particular need related to mission. In a number of ways, small churches can and need to learn to share in the adventure of mission.

We in the affluent West have much to learn from our brothers and sisters in the Two-thirds world about genuine New Testament Christianity, and especially in light of the regular expressions of sacrificial giving and serving which is regularly evidenced in their lives.[9] Even though many of the churches in the Two-thirds world are small, they have a vision which is larger than themselves. Often they tithe to missions, and are regularly sending out missionaries where just a few decades ago, they were on the receiving end. Their overall vision is not maintenance but mission.

Our own church has struggled to keep this important perspective in our own giving and stewardship. The congregation has made it a point to return a tithe of all the giving to missions, so we are looking beyond ourselves and are actively engaged in missions with the poor and the Two-thirds world. Perhaps this can be offered as a model of growth in this vital area of a small church's life.

These are only four possible strategies for assisting the small church in facing its need for financial giving. But where the church can begin to participate in these areas, then self-esteem can be raised, and the emphasis can change from receiving to giving. Then the small church will feel and be blessed.

The Awesome Power of the Tithe[10]

I have saved the discussion of the tithe until the end. Partly because it is sometimes seen as only an ideal, and so not taken seriously. There are, of course, many Christians and indeed small churches who are regular in tithing. But for others, either this is beyond their reach or they have not been taught the exciting possibilites of this approach to finance.

Statistically, according to Lyle Schaller[11], about one third of all Christians 'return' a tithe, and the other two thirds let them. Although we do not have the statistics to indicate what percentages tithe in this country, some sources give us a clue. The recent *Faith in the Countryside* report by the Archbishop's Commission on Rural Areas[12] in addressing the difficult issues surrounding the need for readjustment to stipends for clergy, suggests that the average level of giving in 1988 was a mere £2.19 per week per member. In order to realise their new suggestions and see the churches become more accountable in financial terms to their ministers, an additional 76p per week was needed by each member of the Church of England. Even the addition of such a sum would come nowhere near a tithe by more than a small per cent of the congregations.

A story is told of a small Anglican church where the large brass offering plates were passed around one Sunday evening. They were returned to the vicar almost empty. He took them, held them up to heaven and prayed, 'Lord, we thank you for the safe return of these plates . . .' This humorous anecdote brings a smile, but also reflects a common reality.

It seems possible that many more churches would be in a position to see their ministers released to enjoy their work and realise more fruit in their ministries if the members of the congregation began to again demonstrate the regular and sacrificial nature of Christian discipleship with regard to finance, and specifically tithing.

There is a growing number of people in my congregation who are learning the awesome power of tithing. Not everyone is tithing, and not everyone is able to give regularly at that level at the moment. But the testimonies of blessings received (not always financial), and the sheer joy of being able to give, have encouraged others to begin to trust God with their finances and dethrone the power of money in their lives.

Malachi chapter 3 is a sombre warning of what happens when God's people trivialise God and his demands on their lives. The entire sermon is cast in the context of final judgement. But restoration is promised when men and women begin again to participate with God in his work. The alternative is graphically described as robbing God. This had a real effect on the widow, fatherless and sojourner, along with the Levites who received their living from these gifts.

The lack of tithing in Malachi's day had a profound effect on the provision of those who were dependent on such monies. It equally hindered Israel as a mission people, since their lack of sacrifice limited God's blessings. This has also been true throughout the history of the church and the times of significant revival. We need to recapture this awesome power.

The key to all giving and tithing is faith. The impact of faith can be liberating for churches who are struggling with their finances. To give in faith is also to grow in faith. The very act of giving produces faith. Faith in God to provide the funding as He promised; faith in the God who called this church into being for its witness and mission; faith in the power of the gospel to transform lives, churches, communities, and the world. Faith is central to giving as it is to the whole of our Christian lives.

The small church must be financed in order to be engaged in its ministry and worship. Part of the answer to that funding lies in understanding and valuing the very different approach to finance which the small church holds and how it operates. Another part lies in understanding the vision of the local church and how it relates to the overall economy of God and the ecology of mission. Ultimately finance, along with all other areas of a church's life, emanates from vision inspired by faith—what God is doing and wants to do with his people, and that includes the small church.

NOTES

1. Haddon Robinson 'Money: When You Move To Meddlin', Chapter eight of *Mastering Comtemporary Preaching* by Bill Hybels, Stuart Briscoe, and Haddon Robinson (Multnomah /Christianity Today Inc: Portland, 1989), p 99.
2. During the 1984 visit of Billy Graham in Mission England, the accounts were published and made publically available to demonstrate how the offerings were used. In a similar vein, the recent visit of Bill Hybels and his team from Willow Creek Community Church near Chicago, highlighted their practice of asking visitors and non-churched people not to feel obligated to put money in the offering plates when passed, for this is the responsibility of the Christians present—one way of tackling the perceptions of the unchurched to the money issue.
3. Lyle Schaller, *The Small Church is Different*! (Abingdon: Nashville, 1982), p 18.
4. Anthony Pappas, *Money, Motivation, and Mission in the Small Church* (Judson Press: Valley Forge, 1989), pp 15–16.

5. Schaller, *op cit*, pp 152–161. He offers the following six suggestions: (1) No outside fund-raising activities; (2) a limited number of events agreed upon; (3) one, large annual fund-raising event; (4) setting restrictive time limits, eg one every two years; (5) no limitations; (6)intentional events to invite and involve un-churched people. Each church will need to work out which of these are applicable.

6. Schaller gives no less than 13 possible ways of financing a full-time pastor. I have highlighted only a few obvious ones. See his discussion, *op cit*, pp 92–93

7. One obvious example is the collection taken up by the apostle Paul. He asks the churches in Rome and Corinth to give to the needy believers in Jerusalem. This reflects an interdependence in these missionary churches which is often lacking in our modern churches. On this point, the still valuable older work of Keith F Nickle *The Collection: A Study in Paul's Strategy* [Studies in Biblical Theology No. 48] (W & J Mackay & Co: Chatham, 1966) has much to commend. See especially pp 100–142.

8. See Chapter 10 for further discussion on this point.

9. A helpful overview of the tension between the affluence/ poverty in both financial and spiritual terms between the West and the Two-thirds world can be found in Monica Hill, *Rich Christians, Poor Christians* (Marshall, Morgan and Scott: London, 1989).

10. Two important recent books on this subject are R T Kendall, *Tithing* and Richard Foster, *Money, Sex and Power* (Hodder & Stoughton: London, 1983).

11. Lyle Schaller, *op cit*, pp 65–69; also see the interview with Schaller in *Leadership* entitled 'The changing Focus of Church Finances' Vol 2 No 2, (Spring 1981): pp 12–24. It is here Schaller makes the important distinction between giving a tithe and returning one. For in the semantic use of the word 'return', the implication is clearly evident that the giver understands that everything belongs to God, and he is a responsible steward of it.

12. *Faith in the Countryside* (Churchman Publishing Limited: Worthing, 1990), pp 279–308, esp p 292.

CHAPTER NINE

FACING THE CHALLENGE OF CHANGE

THE SEVEN FINAL WORDS OF A CHURCH: 'We've never done it that way before!'

It was their first ministry in a small rural parish of a few hundred people. A young couple had come to minister with vision, passion, commitment, and a desire to see their new church grow and expand. It would only take a few minor changes: replace the hymn book and service book with something new and modern; motivate the congregation to invite their friends and neighbours; it would be so easy for this church to grow.

What the young family had not counted on was the powerful resistance they encountered at every stage. They had only been there for 3 years, and this church had stood for hundreds. They weren't really part of the community, still considered as 'outsiders' by the small, elderly congregation. Why on earth did they wish to change a church which had proven its faithfulness for centuries in the way things were? Eventually they got the message: change was an enemy and not welcome.

That true story illustrates the reality of introducing change to the small church. There tends to be a built-in resistance to change within the very fabric of the smaller congregation. People who learn to live together for a number of years in the church family quickly form a secure but closed group. The very thing which holds them all together is the experience of things as they have always been. This brings a sense of security and enhances trust. It is very understandable that in such a situation change will not be seen as a friend.

Anthony Pappas has discovered six qualities of the small church and six corresponding attitudes for those involved in the leadership of small churches.[1] These insights will assist us in exploring the issues of change.

The Small Church is a Stable Organisation

To be stable is to be strong, secure and reliable. It can equally mean to be restrained, constant, immoveable, and impervious to change. This dual quality is wonderful as we think about God, but not particularly helpful as we consider the church. Yet the reality of the smaller church is that it is essentially a stable, not a dynamic organisation. A stable group is usually resistant to change for fear of upsetting its stability. Here there is confidence, faithfulness and security.

The small church tends not to rethink its previous patterns of behaviour but repeats them time and time again. This is most obvious in the worship experience of the smaller church. The particular use of liturgical materials, the length of time of the worship services, the styles and types of music and instruments, the appropriate form of attire, all contribute to the feeling of stability. What has worked in the past is used again in the present.

One church in the North East of England has demonstrated this stability in a most interesting way. This particular small Free Church congregation has hand written its order of service, protected it in a plastic cover, and stapled it onto the communion table. The only items which change are the hymns, but the order remains static. For an essentially non-liturgical church, this structure provides a permanence and perpetuity of expression in its worship experience. There is little room for change here.

Although it is difficult, change in this setting is not impossible. Effective leadership will need to recognise that a long-term view of change, with gradual positive steps forward will ultimately bring some freshness. The leader will need to persevere with each step in order to achieve the potential change. A recognition that once any change is in place means it too may

live 'forever' also needs to be realised by leaders wanting to
effect change in the small church.

The Small Church is Primarily Introverted

One of my friends is a collector of comics. On one occasion
when I was visiting him, he took me to a shop which sold
nothing but comics. Everyone who entered the shop was either
buying, selling, or talking about comics. It was like entering a
new and very strange world, since I was neither a collector or
reader of comics. I was amazed that such a world even existed.
But I quickly realised I was not a part of it, only a visitor. I was
not conversant with the language, the stories, the history, the
memories. I was not only an outsider to this world, I equally
felt it too.

The small church can also be a little world to itself. What
happens within the confines of its own boundaries is that which
is essentially important to its members. As with the example of
the comic shop, the world of the small church is both satisfying
and meaningful to those within it. They are a primary group
who care for each other. They have learned to know and
understand each other, to love and care for one another, to
share a common history and experience. This has caused an
internalising of the church, whether conscious or not.

One of the obvious dilemmas which faces all who work with
the smaller church is the problem of objectivity. It is hard for
a group which is single-celled and inward-looking to be aware
of itself as others see it. Thus everything within will feel secure
and business as usual for the members. But for the minister who
is felt to be an outsider, or the visitor to the church, this group
of believers can seem to be a closed circle so that it is difficult
to be accepted or become part of this group.

The leader's role is a crucial one when facing this reality of
the small church. He or she must be willing to accept the
tension of living both inside the church's world as well as having
contact with other realities. Direction and change can occur
because a leader can bring a perspective from outside the
church, coupled with care and compassion as expressed by the

leader's commitment to the church. A voice crying in the wilderness is not nearly as effective as the shepherd's call to his flock.

The Small Church Sees the Past not the Future

'I remember when . . .' is the language of family gatherings, of adults in middle age (especially when talking about music, school, or other involvements in childhood), and small churches. The 'good old days' are now nothing more than cherished but important memories for each of these groups of people. The past affects the present and colours the future.

Within the memory banks of small churches are volumes of stories, narratives, and even a few myths of the 'holy history' of this particular group of Christian believers. These are freely drawn upon to illustrate that there was a time when life in this church was better. The names of the patriarchs and matriarchs of those who have gone on before are recited and recalled as the early beginnings, or special times of blessing and growth, are remembered. The past is what is before the eyes of the small church. This is their home.

Leadership and change are primarily about the future. Not where we have been or even where we are now, but where we want to be. This forward-looking approach, which is essential to all effective leadership, crashes into the wall of the perspectives and values of the small church. Here is a fundamental tension which must be resolved in order to allow needed and desired changes to take place.

The way forward is a move backwards. The past needs to become an ally, not a competitor. By learning to value the past memories of the members, the wise leader can begin to build a bridge into the future. In order to facilitate this, leaders must learn to become conversant with the memories, to listen to all the chatter of the past, to attempt to 'feel' part of this tradition of God's work with this small church. Though we cannot enter a time machine and go back in time, we can listen, watch, and learn to appreciate the past history of our people.

Carl S. Dudley and Douglas Walrath comment:

Congregational history can be mobilized for change when memories are chosen to fit the contemporary challenge and when the energizing spirit of adventure from the past is more important than merely repeating a particular pattern of behavior.[2]

So this does not mean staying in the past. We are not creating museums of faith. Rather, we are finding how the future goals, visions, and direction of the church can be expressed within a framework of continuity. Such a structure will bridge the past, present and future, in ways that the members of the small church can relate to emotionally and intentionally. The small church finds it hard to see the future, and may not really want to. By building this type of bridge, a leader has a way of leading the small church into the future in ways which do not sound foreign or feel unusual or unnatural.

The Small Church Functions Out of Reflex and Habit

Any pastor who has worked in the same small church for a long time will become able to predict fairly accurately how various people will respond to particular issues and traumas. Some will become devasted and discouraged. They will either withdraw and become quiet, or they will cry their frustration and disappointment aloud. Others will press on in a stoic fashion, not letting their feelings be demonstrated to the church community, but within individual conversations their true feelings will be aired. Finally, others will accept and move on, not allowing the present to dislodge them from their pilgrimage of faith and forward movement. People are creatures of habit and tend to respond reflexively.

This response, which is found within individual members of a church, is also mirrored in the life of an entire congregation. The small church is equally a creature of habit and reflex. It senses needs in the environment and then responds in the ways which have a proven record in the past.

Some small churches often respond well to crises. Whether it is a death within the church; a family becoming homeless; a need for food or clothing; in all these ways some churches respond with some immediate aid, prayers, visits, whatever is appropriate. In fact, whatever is habitual for this congregation.

I have experienced some of this response first hand. We have a network of people who are committed to pray at any given notice. With just a phone call to indicate a need for prayer, the message is quickly passed on to the team of people who will pray for the situation. This is both habitual and reflexive. The habit had to be learned. The prayer chain had to be established. This materialised due to a continuing need for prayer and an effective way to get as many people praying as possible. What began as a response to needed prayer now has become part of the identity of our small church.

Because the small church is primarily habitual and functions out of reflex, the implementation of goals and strategies, which are essentially rational by definition, will not be adopted easily. There may indeed be a reflex action and response out of habit to these proposals, but it is likely to be a defeatist response. Yet, goals are essential to all leadership and movement of a church. How do we overcome this apparent stalemate?

The solution is in enabling the church to build up good habits and ingrained behavioural patterns. The key is transformation rather than production. Getting the job accomplished is the objective of setting goals; building up good habits is the objective which is required in the small church. It is still important to accomplish the task and complete the required job, but the church will not respond to this unless it can 'see' it as part of the normal reflexive response out of habit. The effective leader will work long and hard to become comfortable with secondary and indirect activity, but this is the way of the small church.

Relationships Are Key in the Small Church

Many secular (and some Christian) organisations operate on the dictum: 'It's not what you know but who you know.' This statement assumes that the key to successful and growing organisations is in understanding who does what function, who is in charge, and where the buck stops. Those who wield the power are key people. In the smaller church, the dictum is the same but means something different. For the reality is that in many, if not most, small churches, the people you know will be the church gathered together. Relationships are primary, functions are often secondary.

Dudley reminds us that, 'The small congregation is the appropriate size for only one purpose: the members can know one another personally.' He further comments, 'The caring cell church may be defined as a primary group in which the members expect to know, or know about, all other members.'[3]

For the trained pastor, straight out of theological college, the temptation will be to prove oneself by what you know. But this will generally be ineffective, for the model is inadequate for the smaller church. Many members of small churches are primarily interested in knowing if they are loved, accepted, welcomed and part of this family of believers. People are more important than programmes: 'The relationships of life, rather than the functions of the church, top the priority list in the small church.'[4]

This can be evidenced in conversations. One large church discovered that with so many new people being added and visiting, that the first name basis on which they had been operating was no longer effective. Now they often introduce one another in a service with both the Christian and surname along with their appropriate job title. In some small churches, the Christian name is usually all that is given, and other titles or discussions about jobs are not as relevant. I am often introduced as Dan, who is our minister. This is Linda, our worship leader.

In addition, when new people have come into the church, I have found that my members often ask me, 'Who is the person sitting in the chair on the right of Margaret?' This often means, 'What is their name, where do they live, did they like the service, are they likely to come again?' How I'm supposed to know all of this is a mystery to me. But they are seeking ways to establish relationships in order to see if the new people 'fit'.

Relationships are equally important within the body of the church, and often take a lot of work to keep them balanced and maintained. I have experienced more heated debates and raised voices in the small church than perhaps anywhere else. And yet, I have also seen these same people come away as friends afterwards. Perhaps this is because the small church is built on the strength of relationships, and in all good relationships, there is a need for some space for disagreement, debate, and challenge. This means the relationships need to be balanced and liveable. Only then will any needed change be able to be assimilated and acted upon.

Because of this, change will only begin to take place after much time and energy has been invested in people. Tasks will be faced, but only after members come face-to-face with their leaders. 'To know and to be known, to love and to be loved' are essential to the life of the small church. Perhaps this is essentially why the commands and exhortations in the New Testament epistles are written to church members with regard to their relationships with each other.

The Small Church Lives on the Level of Experience

While it is true that both the members of the small church and the large church assess change on the basis of how it will affect them personally, the process for evaluating the impact of change is different.

The larger church tends to propose change on the basis of a planned project. For example, if a larger church wanted to build a new building, they would begin with a small task group to research the need, the costs, the planning, all aspects. This would then be promoted by the leadership over a long period of time, highlighting the benefits as well as the current and future needs for growth and development. Then at a given point, they would ask the congregation to support the decision with prayer, money, and time. The theory would logically move to practice, if all the steps were accepted along the way. This is the model of proposed change.

Smaller churches work on a different level as well as a different model. Here people need to have the suggested changes become part of their experiences. Then they can adequately respond. The changes need to be felt and perceived to be beneficial to the church and to each person. They need to experience the proposal before committing themselves to any change.

During the 1970's, one pastor of an inner city congregation in Birmingham was wrestling with the changing community of people around him, and the apparent rigidity of his own church. In order for real change to take place, he realised that a conversion needed to happen. But this was not just for the hundreds of unchurched who surrounded the building in high tower flats. This also included his church leaders. They needed to realise the distance between the life of the church and the people in their community. The answer to this dilemma was very surprising.

This church pastor encouraged his leaders to go with him door-to-door calling. When they shared in this work, the leaders experienced the gulf which existed between the church and the local community of people. They soon realised the church members and the people in their community were worlds apart. This felt and perceived distance helped to create the value of positive and needed change. Such a change could never have been primarily accomplished by the minister teaching or preaching about reaching the lost. Rather, he knew the gap had to be felt, to become personal, before the small church leaders were able to face the implication that change was not only needed but essential.

In another small church, one leader stood as a man in transition. He had been like a gate keeper, forming a bridge from the old dying congregation of the past, with all its traditions and values, and the emerging new church of younger people whom the Lord was adding. Like the husk which protects the wheat while it is growing, this man was protecting the church during this time of transition. When this key leader died, the husk fell away, the wheat was revealed, and a new church was revealed, which had been forming for many years. It would have been impossible without his love and protection for the needed change to materialise. He kept his watch at the gate, guarding as well as nurturing, until the time was right for the gates to be swung wide and the new life expressed. Key people act as a link with the past. They protect the emerging new life which is beginning to develop. Change came gradually but helpfully with the aid of this local church leader.

This illustrates the importance of finding the key people in each small church. While it would be ideal to have the entire church working in total partnership to effect change, the reality is that the consensus model is not very effective in seeking to bring planned change. The small church leaders in the above examples did not bring everyone along in the change process at the same time. Instead they located key people, those who were trusted by all and who were willing to personally embrace needed change. Finding these key leaders (and they are not always the recognised ones with leadership titles), getting to know them, and working closely with them will effect change more quickly than any other approach within the small church.[5]

Change takes time, energy, and commitment.[6] The wise leader of the smaller church knows that even Jesus saw little change in the lives of his closest disciples after three intense years of living together in community with each other. But once the change took place, these men turned the world upside down.

The small church does often resist change, or at least this is how it seems. In the words of Tony Pappas:

> The small church world does not change easily. Nurturing progress in a small church is a difficult job. It takes time. It takes love. It takes blood, sweat and tears. If you aspire to move a small church congregation, be prepared to perspire.[7]

Once we begin to understand and appreciate that the church has its own distinct set of qualities, as well as attitudes with regard to change, we will be in a better position to assist in the change process, becoming what Lyle Schaller calls the change agent.[8] But as Schaller also warns, change agents need to be careful. They may end up teaching a seminar somewhere on 'How to cut your own throat.'[9]

Notes

1. Anthony Pappas, *Entering the World of the Small Church*, (The Alban Institute: Washington, DC, 1988) pp 53–74. For much of the following discussion, I have freely borrowed from Pappas' material.

2. Carl S Dudley and Douglas Alan Walrath, *Developing Your Small Church's Potential*, (Judson Press: Valley Forge, 1989) p 87.

3. Carl S Dudley, *Making the Small Church Effective*, p 35.

4. Lyle E Schaller, *The Small Church is Different*, p 32.

5. Gordon MacDonald, in his celebrated book, *Restoring Your Spiritual Passion* (Oliver Nelson: Nashville, 1986), pp 71–91, speaks of how he learned after many years that people fell into five categories. These are: VRP (Very Resourceful people—those who ignite our passion); VIP (Very Important People—those who share our passion); VTP (Very Trainable People—those who catch our passion); VNP (Very Nice People—those who enjoy our passion); and finally VDP (Very Draining People—those who sap our passion). He had to realise that only by investing time in the key people would his church become really effective. Unfortunately, he had attempted to invest in everyone, especially the final group who made the most noise and required the most time and attention. The first three groups were being either ignored or left to their own devices. Once MacDonald shifted his approach to equally investing in those who would help to develop him, rather than just drain and take from him, then his ministry became more effective.

6. There are various studies which deal with the importance of change. I have narrowed the discussion in this chapter with the small church particularly in mind. However, there is much to benefit and learn from other wider views. The reader is directed to some of the following studies for further development on the theme of change:

   E M Rogers and F F Shoemaker, *The Communication of Innovations* (Collier MacMillian: New York, 1971); John Finney, *Understanding Leadership* (Daybreak: London, 1989), pp 139–143; Eddie Gibbs, *Followed or Pushed* (Marc Europe: Bromley, 1987), pp 166–186.

7. Pappas, *op cit*, p 55.

8. Lyle E Schaller, *The Change Agent: The Strategy of Innovative Leadership* (Abingdon: Nashville, 1972).

9. This is the title of the first chapter of Lyle Schaller's book quoted above in note 4.

CHAPTER TEN

VISION: WHERE ARE WE GOING?

Where there is no vision, the people perish. (Prov 29:18, AV)
'Boy, I got vision and the whole world wears bifocals' Butch
Cassidy in the film *Butch Cassidy and the Sun Dance Kid*.
'You see things as they are and ask "why?" But I dream things
that never were and ask "why not?"' George Bernard Shaw.
'I have a dream . . .' Martin Luther King, Jr.

Whether in the worlds of business, politics, family, community,
special interest groups, or the church, there will be some kind
of vision, one which initiated the group and gave it a reason to
exist and to carry out its life and work.

But immediately with regard to the smaller church, we are
faced with the important question 'whose vision?'. Is it the vision
of the original church and its members, no matter how many
generations have come and gone? Or the vision of the current
group of leaders, or the laity, who often have at least one if not
many visions? Or the vision of the minister, who will often bring
an 'outside' perspective? Or the vision of the denomination or
oversight group, or of the community or culture?

VISION IS THE ABILITY TO SEE THE FUTURE WHICH
DOES NOT YET EXIST AND TO BE MOTIVATED
AND EMPOWERED TO MAKE IT A REALITY IN THE
PRESENT.

Even though many small churches have lost contact with
their original vision, it was nevertheless part of their own

history, and helped to establish that particular congregation. But churches, as with other organisations, must move ahead. Their vision will either have to lead them or be changed and adapted in some way in order to provide motivation and direction.

Leadership and Vision

One of the primary places where vision is brought to birth, developed, articulated, and demonstrated is with the leadership of any church. This includes both the minister and the lay leadership, and may well also include others within the congregation without specific titles of leadership and authority.

Many contemporary writers on Christian leadership have concluded that the place of a key leader (minister/pastor/elder) has been demonstrated to be of critical importance.[1] For example, Tom Marshall, in his excellent book *Understanding Leadership* speaks about the crucial place of leaders and vision in these words:

> The first essential characteristic of leaders is that they are going somewhere, in other words they are aiming at goals or objectives that lie in the future. Their interest therefore is in what is to come rather than in what is past, in the possibilities and opportunities that lie on the time horizon rather than the things that have already been accomplished. Leaders, in other words, are always on the way, they are heading towards objectives, aiming at targets and reaching out for things that are ahead of them.[2]

The Biblical models of Abraham (with the vision of a night sky full of stars and the promise of a nation); Moses (with a vision to get the people out of Egypt and into the promised land); Nehemiah (to rebuild the walls of Jerusalem); Peter (with a vision on the rooftop to change the direction of the church); and finally John in the Apocalypse (of the future new heaven and earth and the establishment of the Kingdom of God) also help us to realise that visions are crucial to leadership, since God often uses vision to assist in bringing about his purposes.

But if vision is to be effective, it cannot remain within the confines of leadership. It must be translated to others. Herein lies the problem for the small church and its leadership. Resistance to the vision will inevitably be the initial response. The leader who wishes to help the small church into its future will need to translate the vision in ways which will allow the congregation to face the challenges of change and be led forward without losing its sense of well-being.

Sharing the vision

One of the tensions the small church leader faces is that his or her vision may not be the same as that of the church. If the pastor's vision is to evangelise the local area, and the church is more concerned with keeping the status quo and maintaining what it already has, there is not only tension but a dichotomy of vision. Unless visions are shared, there will be much frustration and heartache in the working out of the vision in ministry which will inevitably be unfruitful.

Living the vision

Leadership always leads by example, and it is of fundamental importance that the minister not only articulates a vision but seeks faithfully to live the vision with honesty and determination before the people of God. In this way, there is a living model of what this vision is to be. But this is not only for one person, since the entire church must also seek to emulate this in their life, worship and work for the Kingdom of God. Each member should help the other to achieve their own demonstration of the vision in practice, not only in principle. In this sense, vision is much more caught than taught.

Empowering the vision

People easily forget. Because of this, it is vital that the leader assists in empowering the vision into the lives of his or her people.[3] Some have suggested this could be done through regular communication such as frequently preaching on the vision, or publicising it in the newsheets or magazines, as well as at particular times in services. Keeping it before the people will assist them in not forgetting it, but actually absorbing it as part of themselves. Whatever ways are chosen, the people need to believe that this vision is answering the questions of why and how—why are we here and how do we express this now?

Owning the vision

For the small church leader, this part of leadership is most crucial. Unless the body of believers sees the vision as theirs, it will automatically be rejected as something outside of their frame of reference and thus 'foreign'. Taking time to listen to the vision of the original leaders can help to facilitate this process, especially if the vision can be shown to be similar or compatible to the life of the church in previous years.[4]
In the words of Dudley and Walrath:

> Congregations that intentionally affect their times have a sense of purpose and a plan; they have a vision of what God is calling them to be and to do. Their vision is often grounded in the biblical promise and articulated only by a minority of members, but many more members feel the excitement and share the commitment. Thus the person who articulates the appropriate vision for the congregation becomes the leader and is both the cause and the result of a mobilized church; both the church and the leader are mutually empowered in the process. Pastors often report feeling a 'second ordination' when the vision they have suggested is accepted and absorbed into the life of the congregation.[5]

Leadership which can share, live, empower, and help their church to own the vision of God for their congregation will be most effective in their task of leading this people of God. But the question which still remains is how to do it.

Making the Vision a Reality

Creating confidence in the present

Speak to any small church leader and you will begin to hear comments about the church's apparent preoccupation with survival, maintenance and the past. Equally talk to many small church members and you will also hear conversations of a similar nature. Unfortunately, many leaders become frustrated and disillusioned with their ministry because they have missed an important distinction. Even though the church does often speak about survival (how will we pay these bills?), maintenance (we don't have enough helpers, we always have the same people), and the past (I remember when . . .), this is only the common language of experience of the small church.

Those in smaller churches often have very little confidence in the present. This often includes the leadership. Yet, this is the place to begin to see vision become a reality. The key task is to build self-esteem and worth. Larger churches seem to deal with the present much more effectively, but they generally have healthier views of themselves and of their capabilities with the power of the Holy Spirit. Small churches often look through rose-coloured glasses at the present by means of the past.

Recently I attended a national event held in a small church. This particular congregation had recently celebrated close to 100 years of life and witness in a changing urban environment. One of the original leaders, who well remembered days of blessing, began his welcome very apologetically to the gathered delegates about the smallness of the congregation. But he equally spoke, with a twinkle in his eye, of the better days when the church was fuller, and even had a vision of it returning to this state. For him, a full church was a sign of success. The present small body of believers was a reason to apologise.[6]

This small church is typical of many others who do not have positive self-esteem and worth. The issue is how can we build these needed qualities in the present? The answer often comes from outside the church, from someone who cares but can equally be objective. This is the responsibility of leadership, and especially the role of clergy and ministers.

Those within cannot help but be self-critical and focus on the negative present and the golden age of the past. The trained leader can offer a positive evaluation and emphasise the good things of this small church. When this begins to take place, and the leader's comments are taken on board by the membership, then the present becomes a new place, a place of confidence in what God is doing, what has already been achieved and is in place at the moment. This then will begin to create good self-esteem and positive worth for the small church.

The only danger is when the trained leader becomes too much a part of the small church so the objective edge becomes blurred. When this happens, then the vision is lost. The leader becomes one of the led, and cannot offer this vital role of enhancing the value of the present. In the wise counsel of Tony Pappas:

> The wise small church leader must be able to live in and enjoy the small church world but must not be trapped in it. He or she must be part of the people in order to have his or her leadership accepted and appropriate, but not so much a part of the small church world as to offer no impetus to greater faithfulness.[7]

It is here, in the present, that leaders and church members must begin to work together. For many small churches, survival is the only thing on the horizon. There may be many and various stories of days of old when things were better, but the hard core reality of the present is where vision must be taken on board. Once confidence can be established by a growing positive self-esteem, then the first step towards a new vision can be realised.

Celebrating the past

All churches have memories, no matter how long they have been in existence. As churches grow older, the potential pool of memories a church can draw from should in theory be deep and wide. Unfortunately, with the mix of faith and human nature which makes up all Christian believers and churches, there are relativly few memories that we hold on to. The 'good old days' scenario is often prominent in many small churches, especially those churches which can still recall from some of the members what a church full of people, excitement, and vision was like.

This second step of vision building, recalling how things used to be, can actually become a hindrance to creating vision. If the members believe that things can never be like they were in the golden age of the past, then the church will become blinkered from any new vision or change. These memories then become a means of discouragement. Instead of creating a positive response of faith and vision, they can act as a wedge of unbelief and stalemate. On the other hand, memory can be used affirmatively to remind people that the issues of the past, before the good old days, were similar to how they are now, and if some of the 'holy history' of the church is readily available, this can be used to infuse and empower vision in a God who worked in the past and can work again. These memories need to be celebrated regularly to rebuild confidence and remind people of God's great faithfulness.

One inner-city church leader who has attempted to strengthen his small congregation is Raymond Bakke. He used memories of the past to help create new vision in his inner city church by reminding the people who were resistant to growth, change and vision that the early expressions of faith and witness were similar or the same to his proposals for the present.[8] He was illustrating that there was nothing new under the sun. This is one way of enabling a stagnant small church which has a treasure house of memories to access these for movement and growth. But it takes a wise leader to take the time to discover and make use of this heritage of faith.

Anthony Pappas offers these words of wisdom:

> Some of the most effective leadership acts a small church pastor can perform are to become a history buff, read up on the struggle of faith of the parish, sit at the feet of some of the older members, and play 'Remember when. . .'[9]

He argues that the past is in fact an ally if we use it correctly. When a leader begins to use memories as a means of empowerment, then the vision will become once again what God is doing and wants to do, rather than what he once did.

The past quickly accumulates within a congregation, no matter how long the church has been in existence. I am working with a relatively young small church, and there is not such a large pool of memories to draw from. But we have just recently celebrated 10 years of my induction as minister. Celebrating this event has helped the church to focus positively on when God called the church into being, of how He has faithfully provided in the past decade, as well as a means to help recreate a vision which will enable the church to focus on its strengths and move forward into tomorrow. [10]

Creating space for God to work (Enhancing the future)

In order for the smaller church to move forward, a strategy for facing the future needs to be developed and implemented. The following checklist can be useful in facing the future:

1. Have We Listened?

Peter Brierley suggests that churches should set aside at least a day together to pray and think through where God is leading them and where they want to go.[11] Small steps will be important for the smaller church. Not everyone will want to be part of this process initially. Perhaps a few church leaders or key members could meet for prayer, or just note that this day is being given over for prayer and listening to God, to regather later to share what they have heard from God.

One small church I know was wrestling with low self-esteem and no forward direction. There had been a series of internal difficulties over the previous few years, the attendance and offerings were quite low, and people were generally tired and demotivated. They spent a day together away from their neighbourhood in another scenic town. Their time of prayer revealed their strengths and weaknesses, but it also created some space for God to move among them as they tried to listen to God and one another. For this congregation, listening brought healing. They are now back on track and beginning to grow again.

2. What do we do well?

As we have already suggested, many small churches suffer from low self-esteem. They usually see what they cannot do or achieve. If a church can focus and identify one or two areas of ministry which they are very competent and blessed in and concentrate on these, then this will improve their self-esteem as well as help the church to become known for these areas of service.

Our own small church has strengths in our Sunday worship, in our Bible study and teaching, but we are weak in evangelism and administration. We have sought to continue to develop and improve these two areas of strength, and are now in the process of identifying ways we can deal with the weaknesses. This helps to keep things focused without feeling regularly defeated.

3. What can we celebrate?

We have already mentioned the importance of celebration, especially key annual events and special moments in the life of the church (such as anniversaries). This is especially helpful where a church has lost its sense of direction and vision and only sees the past with heartache. New memories need to be created and celebrated on a regular basis.

Giving thanks to God for his provision, his faithfulness, and his leading is good for every church. Every small step which meets with success and brings a sense of achievement can help lead to larger steps of faith and trust. The entire biblical narrative echoes this pattern of God's history, and each congregation is a part of His divine plan.

4. What are our immediate goals?

Vision is always a way of seeing into the future. We have already indicated the importance of leadership which directs a church into the life God has in store for it. Each congregation is unique and special. Learning God's purposes and leading the flock into new pastures is crucial for growth and development, even in small areas.

It is imperative to assist each church to establish goals which are congruent with the will of God and which give practical direction to the vision (Chapter 12 will deal with goal setting in more detail). For the small church, the essential issue is working on some immediate, short term goals. These need to be identified and endorsed by the members. They can be as simple as recognising one area of strength and encouraging ways of reinforcing it.

In setting goals for the future, there are inevitably certain tensions which the small church needs to take into account.

Tensions to be Faced

Continuity and discontinuity

The small church receives much of its values from continuity with the past. In contrast, the larger church almost revels in discontinuity. A larger church might deal with the past with an almost flippant attitude. 'Things may have been bad, but they will change now.' This is primarily due to the importance of goal setting. Goals imply discontinuity. Things are not currently acceptable. Change needs to take place. Discontinuity is the welcome advocate for bringing desired change.

The small church is more comfortable with continuity. There is nothing wrong, things are acceptable to us. We've always done it this way, why change? (I have already covered this in Chapter 9). This tension must be taken into account before vision can begin to become a process towards a new reality.

Quantative and qualitative growth

Numerical growth, new programmes and development, setting and meeting goals is the language of the larger church. Quantative growth is crucial to the larger church's vision, as is the quality of its programmes and worship. The small church is primarily relational. Therefore its dialect will reflect this aspect. There you will find such expressions as deeper fellowship with one another, caring for each other, learning to mature in your walk with Christ—this is the small church's speech. Quantity is less important than quality of relationship. Goals imply that with growth, this aspect might be lost. Quantity is therefore a tension within the small church. We want the family to grow, but we still want it to be the family.

Spirituality

The spirituality issue is a very real tension. This is partly to do with the embarrassment factor. For example, some small church worship is embarrassing for both visitors and members alike. Those visiting don't understand what is taking place, everything is assumed. The quality of the music or the preaching can be poor or mediocre. The members can be frustrated since they want something better, but the emphasis is on participation at the cost of performance.

This is often not so in the larger church. Good music, strong biblical preaching, quality leading, an attractive building or atmosphere is often part of the fabric of the larger church's worship experience. This public aspect of spirituality is one area of significant tension.

In addition, some small church members have been faithfully attending their church out of habit for many years. The question of their personal walk with Jesus has little to do with them going to church. They go because they have always gone. The implication of goals and change suggests that they must face up to their own spirituality, or lack of it. This can easily be resisted by keeping things as they are.

Boundaries

For centuries, long before there were Ordnance Survey Maps, a custom which was celebrated annually in local parishes was the beating of the bounds. This all-aged event was used to mark out the boundaries by having the gathered congregation walk around them on a particular day. Older members would communicate knowledge to the younger, so they could know their boundaries.

Even though the practice of beating the boundaries has ceased to exist, there are known and felt boundaries for each local church. This can cause some tensions. The primary and indeed secondary focus of small congregations can often be on the group inside the church building, or at least the group considered to belong to this church. Large churches direct their gaze beyond themselves to others—both the unchurched in the community and in other parts of the world. But the small church has its primary sight set on itself. Thus the wider diversity of church life and expression is woefully lacking, and the sense of mission is not apparent. The small church has well-defined boundaries of who is in and who is out, whereas the larger church is often pushing against these in order to increase the number of members.

All of these tensions are ones which each small church must work out in order to facilitate a vision to lead into the future. The question of 'where are we going?' is crucial to the life and future of each church. The small church is no exception. Leaders and laity will need to work together in order to dream possibilities and realities of where God might take them.

NOTES

1. See, for example the comments in C Peter Wagner, *Leading Your Church to Growth*, pp 194–195 ('The vision for where God wants the church to go usually is channelled through the pastor.'); Peter Brierley, *Vision Building*, (Hodder and Stoughton: London, 1989) pp 164–165 ('The essential source, under God, of a vision is in the heart of the leader, a person who possesses the mental power to create a vision and a practical ability to bring it about . . . ultimately the leader has to decide on the vision.'); and Paul Beasley-Murray, *Dynamic Leadership* p 183 ('The church is an army on the move, and what an army needs is a leader with a sense of strategy. Vision is of the essence of leadership.') as a sample of recent Christian literature on leadership and vision.

   I might point out, however, that much of this language is large church dialect. The larger church usually looks to the pastor for vision. The smaller church, as I will attempt to demonstrate in this chapter, can have many visions, and is often resistant to a vision seen to be from outside itself.

2. Tom Marshall, *Understanding Leadership*, (Sovereign World Ltd: Chichester, 1991), p 9.

3. See the helpful discussion from a business perspective in James A Belasco, *Teaching the Elephant to Dance* (Hutchinson Business Books Ltd: London, 1990), pp 98–126.

4. Raymond Bakke illustrates how in his small inner city church there was resistance to many of his visions until he demonstrated that what he wished to achieve had been nearly identical with the vision and procedures of the church in its infancy and its leaders. This link with the older generation built upon the strengths of their work and

helped to build a bridge to the present and the future vision. *The Urban Christian*, (Marc Europe: Bromley, 1987), pp 89–91.

5. Carl S Dudley and Douglas Alan Walrath, *Developing Your Small Church's Potential* (Judson Press: Valley Forge, 1989), p 88.

6. Of course, many members of small churches are not in fact apologetic, but very positive about belonging to 'Our' church. This is the conclusion of Carl S. Dudley *Making the Small Church Effective* (Abingdon Press: Nashville, 1978), p 29; Schaller takes a slightly different view and speaks about the importance of building the self-esteem of the small church (*The Small Church is Different*, pp 58–60). These are not mutually exclusive and can often be found working together in any given church.

7. Pappas, *Entering the World of the Small Church*, p 56.

8. *Op cit*, pp 88–93. Because his church had become so debilitated, along with this use of what he calls 'having a functional memory', the church worked and worshipped for one month then had a celebration of what God was doing among them. In this way, he was building a new memory bank and after a year, the church had only fruitful memories to move them forward.

9. Pappas, *Entering the World of the Small Church*, pp 77–80.

10. Lyle Schaller, *Hey, That's Our Church!* (Abingdon: Nashville, 1975), pp 187–192 on the importance of celebrating key events in the life of the church.

11. Peter Brierley, *Vision Building*, p 135–137.

CHAPTER ELEVEN

THE COMMUNITY OF FAITH

The writer Carl S. Dudley poses a fascinating question, 'If small churches are such a caring cell, then why is there so much tension between pastor and people?'[1] We have noted in an earlier chapter the insight of Lyle Schaller that small churches tend to resist the leadership of a professional pastor.[2] Sometimes that resistance is so severe that a particular congregation becomes known among denominational leaders as a 'minister killer'. Throughout the 1980's I served as the chairperson of the ministerial placements committee of my denomination. I noted that throughout that time the congregations which were the most vocal in expressing their need for a minister were in fact those congregations which were usually thought of as one of the 'minister killer' brigade. Interestingly, the committee, (probably without being aware of it) tended to spend far more time and effort finding clergy for these 'killer congregations' than they did for other less vocal congregations who had a good track record in pastor/people relationships.

What gives rise to these 'can't manage without a minister, will always argue with a minister' scenarios? The clue lies in a remark that Dudley quotes from one family in a small church. They noted, 'There's a lot of management in our small congregation, and most of it seems to be aimed at keeping the pastor under control.'[3] Those who are in power in a small church recognise their need to have access to skills that they do not have, but at the same time will strongly resist those same skills being used to change the small church that they know and love.

The conflict inherent in such a tension finds its most direct expression in relation to the issue of programme. We might even go so far as to say that one of the critical differences between the small church and the larger church is that of the church programme. Larger churches operate effective programmes, small churches specialise in the intimacy of relationships. I am not saying that larger churches have no intimate relationships or that small churches have no programmes, but there is a clear difference of priority.

Here lies the nub of the problem between the small church and their pastor. A professional minister is usually trained to operate programmes. Even if the theological college that he or she attended was not strong on practical ministries, most clergy will have had some further training in the operation of church programmes. Certainly, clergy are often aware of the successful programmes of other churches and are usually curious to know more about them. The books that clergy buy are more often to do with resource ideas than with theology. The conferences that achieve the highest attendances from clergy are heavily oriented towards a 'how to do it' theme.

We can go further and claim that many local church leaders call a clergyman specifically because they hope for some programme input. 'We need a Sunday School in order to reach the children in our area', or 'We need something for the young mums in the neighbourhood', or even, 'We're nor sure what we want, but somehow we don't seem to be meeting the needs of our community'. There is a tension for the leaders of a small church between wanting to continue as they are and yet knowing that some growth will be needed if the church is to stay open. 'No-one ever visits our church', is the sad confession of many small churches. The introduction of some activity is seen as a means of changing that position and producing enough growth to allow life to continue. The professional clergy person is seen, whether consciously or not, to be the means of introducing such activity. New programmes can be viewed with suspicion. Therefore, any programmes that the new minister brings will be very carefully monitored and, if necessary, resisted.

So how can a minister, called to serve a small church, chart these potentially stormy waters and succeed in building the community of faith? It is clear that even though at times the small church does need to introduce a degree of programming in order for its life to be healthy, there needs to be a conscious attempt to adjust the style of programme. The very nature of most church programmes is that they are targeted to reach particular homogenous groups and that they therefore require fairly substantial levels of manpower and training in order for them to operate effectively. For example, Sunday Schools usually operate on the basis of a variety of age groups. Materials are produced for small groups of particular ages. The Sunday School teacher training that most clergy will have seen will tend to be designed for such a situation. But in the small church, there will not be sufficient teachers to operate a programme for the full age range. There may only be one person who is gifted and able to work with Sunday School pupils, and they may not feel able to cope with a single large group composed of many ages. The same kind of difficulty applies to programmes regardless of the age group at which they are aimed.

Carl S. Dudley points out that the answer to such a dilemma begins by looking at the different expectations of the pastor and the people, especially with regard to the question of success.[4] The professional minister defines success as the degree to which the church is able to provide something for everyone. That is the conclusion towards which clergy training pushes him or her. However, the members of the small church look elsewhere for their definition of success. Dudley comments:

> For a real program, everyone is present. An almost real program may not be attended by everyone, but all who are absent will hear about it before nightfall. When everyone comes to everything, pastors do not need to plan and push something different for each age group and interest center in the church. Such program divisions are seen as divisive by members of the caring cell.[5]

Operating fewer programmes, but ones where there will be a high level of participation, can help to remove much pressure, and thus potential conflict. Programme pressure is often a major reason for the pace of clergy turnover. Frustration at an apparent inability to maintain a successful programme may lead a minister to conclude that their ministry is either unappreciated or at best that they have made the contribution that realistically they can offer. They will begin to look for another, and probably larger, church. The exhaustion level of a congregation which has tried to keep up with a programme will also determine the length of an interregnum. Dudley notes:

> One denominational executive who helps small churches in their search for pastors has become particularly sensitive to symptoms of exhaustion. He claims that he can predict the length of time a small congregation will take before they call the next pastor. He has calculated that the time between pastorates is directly related to the number of programs that the last pastor initiated: the more programs the longer the interval.[6]

The key to building the community of faith in the small church lies in selecting a small number of programmes and designing them in such a way that they maximise the level of participation. Reading the 'pace' or 'rhythm' of the small church accurately so that burn out is not produced will be critical in lessening the potential for conflict between pastor and people.

So far we have looked at some of the principles that help us to understand the rather different way in which the small church operates its programmes. But these principles need to be understood in relation to some actual ingredients in the life of the small church. The ingredients themselves are the common building blocks of every church regardless of size, but the way in which they operate in the small church needs to be examined.

Worship

Having been brought up as a child of the 1960's, I am perhaps a little hesitant to admit that I enjoy *Songs of Praise*, but I do! I like to see a full church with many hundreds of people giving full voice to some of the great hymns of the church. The colour, the vitality, the diversity represented in some of the better broadcasts can be inspiring. However, the downside of such inspiration is that it can produce a sense that this is what every good worship service should feel, sound and look like.

The small church is required to be involved in a regular act of public worship without the resources available to *Songs of Praise* or to a large church. How can the small church engage in worship that is both intimate and worthy of the description? Three aspects sum up the difference between the large and small church in worship.

Participation

The large church in worship is concerned with quality and that almost always requires specialisation. The small church is not as concerned with quality as it is with producing a sense of family. The signal for the start of services in many small churches is not the time on the clock, but who is present. I have attended a number of small churches where the members can tell you who will come, at what times and in what order. When certain key people have arrived, then it is time to start the service.

The desire for participation in terms of the presence of people can be extended to represent a considerable strength for the small church. A worship committee which meets on a regular basis to plan the worship can help to enhance the sense of worship and significantly increase the degree of participation in the services. A rota for readers, those who will pray and participate in other ways, can be a useful tool for producing very high levels of involvement in the services over a period of time. It will not necessarily enhance the quality of the worship, (although that might be an unexpected by-product), but it will increase the sense of ownership and family.

Simplicity

If the large church needs variety to help its worship live, then the small church needs simplicity. That is not identical to sameness. Indeed one of the problems of the small church in worship lies in the tendency to become stuck in a particular routine. But variety in the small church can often feel like an imposed gimmick, another one of the minister's programme ideas that has to be endured so that we can get back to normal as soon as possible. However, small changes that are simple in their execution and not too demanding of the congregation can be extraordinarily effective in bringing fresh life to the small church at worship. The best innovations will centre on the contributuions that members of the congregation bring as expressions of the family life of the church. A poem that someone in the congregation has written, a simple prayer of thanks for better health or the provision of a job. These are understandable to the small church community.

Expectation

Attendance at worship in the small church can easily become a duty. It is attendance that expresses membership, belonging and a sense of place in the family of the small church. However, true worship is more than duty. It is also delight at being in the presence of God as well as with each other. I have been in some small churches where the worship has almost become a celebration of each other's company to the point where the God whom we worship becomes an unwelcome outsider. An important goal for worship in the small church is to constantly introduce a sense of awe and wonder that the Creator of the universe, the God of Israel, the one who is also present in cathedrals, comes to meet with us. There may well be those in your small church who have the gift, by use of a few simple words, to enhance that sense of wonder. They may never preach, lead, pray or even read the lessons but they may have such a gift. These are precious people and we need to look for them and encourage them.

The Incorporation of New Members

Every small church leader and member will tell you that they would like to see the church grow. They would like to see some new, especially younger members, those who will help to share the workload in the chuch. The congregation would like to see more members to help take the pressure off the finances. Yet in practice, despite the expression of a genuine desire to grow, the small church rarely does grow. There are good reasons why this is the case. Not the least of these reasons relates to the simple fact that when the members of the small church tell you that they would like to have more members, they mean certain types of new members. Those who will 'fit'.

Most of those who might be available to join a particular small church will tend not to fit very easily and so will not find a ready welcome. I remember the comment of an older member in a small church that I once pastored. Something like four new people had been added to a church of around thirty people in the previous year. 'I just don't know anyone in this church anymore', she complained. What she meant was that she no longer knew everyone and she couldn't easily see how she could come to know those who had joined recently because they were very different in age, class and race to herself.

Carl S. Dudley expresses this dilemma very well when he says:

> The small church is already the right size for everyone to know, or know about, everyone else. This intimacy is not an accident. The essential character of the small church is this capacity to care about people personally. The small church cannot grow in membership size without giving up its most precious appeal, its intimacy.[7]

So is it possible for the small church to attract, receive and incorporate new members into their intimate circle of friendship? Writing in the same book, Dudley notes that the best metaphor to describe the process of someone joining the small church is that of 'adoption'. He writes:

> When new members join a large-church activity, they accept a common goal that holds that group together. In such activity groups, the new member often shares in defining and creating the common future. But adoption looks in the other direction, not to the future but to the past. The new member is adopted into the family history. The adoptee must absorb the values of the church, just as the church absorbs the new member.[8]

Unlike the large church, which may offer a membership class and even a new member reception, the small church operates a more informal process. Dudley argues that the process of adoption is facilitated by means of 'gatekeepers' and 'patriarchs/matriarchs'.[9] These people are often not the same as those who comprise the formal leadership of the congregation. Gatekeepers are those who like to talk and to welcome people. They notice when people are not present and make inquiries about them. Patriarchs and matriarchs are those who know the history of the church well and who will share it with the newcomer once they feel confident that the newcomer is likely to appreciate the values that these stories represent. The telling of these stories is more important in incorporating a new member into the small church than any formal membership enrolment process. Such stories help to initiate the new arrival into the life and history of the church.

Discipleship

The making of disciples is coming ever more strongly onto the agenda of the church in the Western world. The issue has become more urgent as the culture in which the church operates becomes less and less obviously Christian. Larger churches have tended to respond to this challenge by making their baptismal, or confirmation or church membership classes a much more significant part of their church life. In other words, the response of the larger church is both programmatic and related in some way to church membership. Such an approach will not be helpful to the small church. First because, as we have already noted, the small church does not thrive on programmes and secondly because the means by which people join the small church are much more informal than in the large church.

Yet it is crucial for the small church to address the area of discipleship. The small church, much more than the large church, has a tendency to attract new members through the strength of its relationships and the sense of family belonging. Yet it is all too easy for such warmth and support to become more important than faith as a motivation for belonging to the small church. At this level, the small church can be merely an effective club for those who need a high level of support and sense of belonging in a hostile society. Worship then becomes simply something that the club members do together but is not really as important as the time of chatting afterwards. A strong sense of the need to disciple every member of the congregation will help to prevent the small church becoming a small social club.

Since most members of the small church seem to 'drift in' rather than join in a more formal sense, how can discipleship take place? Three pointers might be worth considering. First, it is still possible for the small church which is growing to hold church membership classes. Unlike the large church, the classes may not coincide with the moment that people actually join the church on a formal basis. But it is possible to hold an annual class for those who have joined the church in the previous year or two. Such a series will be more effective if some of those who are patriarchs/matriarchs are included in the teaching team. Indeed, it might even be possible for the whole event to be led by lay people. The effect of this approach will be to produce change in the leaders of the church as they consider again the basis of their faith. Further it will deepen the sense that these newcomers are becoming part of the church rather than remaining as the disciples of the new minister who, just as the minister never truly belongs, will also never truly be part of the small church.

Secondly, the effective use of the pastoral office will be the means of imparting much discipleship training. Unlike the larger church where the level of pastoral interface between pastor and people is rather limited, the minister of the small church has an opportunity to know his flock well and, in effect, to devise an informal and individual discipleship approach for every member.

Thirdly, much useful discipleship training can take place in the context of the discovery of gifts and ministries.[10] In one sense the goal of all discipleship is to see each believer operating in the area of their ministry or task. However, that goal has a particular danger for the believer in the small church. Task has a strong social meaning in the small church because it helps to establish place and belonging. However, task in a discipleship context needs to express gifting regardless of place. For example, suppose a person is clearly gifted in the leading of worship. In a large church it is not too difficult for a relative newcomer to the church to be used in such a capacity. The reaction of the large church to such a development might well be 'How fortunate we are to have attracted such a member'. However, in the small church, the reaction to someone who is a relatively new member (say two years or less), leading the worship will be something along the lines of 'But they've only been here five minutes'. They have not yet established both place and belonging.

The leader of a small church needs to keep a clear distinction in mind when helping to locate believers in their ministry. It is a difficult tension to live with, but ministry needs to express gifting and not just place within a congregation.

Leadership Development

In the same way that there is a difference between the larger and the small church in the way that people join the church, there is a clear difference between the way in which leaders are developed. The large church tends to look at leadership development in a programmatic way. Many have either developed their own leadership training programmes, or they will send key potential leaders to be trained through a variety of courses and schemes. In any case, with or without formal training, it is much easier to develop leaders in the context of a programme that already exists. The large church will tend to have such programmes, the small church may not.

The small church benefits more from generalists than from specialists and it is much more difficult to train a generalist for the very simple reason that most people's gifts are rather specific. So how can the minister of a small church, who will probably be a generalist, develop and train leaders?

The model for leadership training in the small church is not the programme but the personal relationship between the minister and those whom he is seeking to train. It is therefore very likely that those who are trained will have joined the church under the ministry of those that are doing the training. Such training takes time and necessitates the trainer being around for some time. The minister of the small church who does not have a long ministry may only be able to develop a very few leaders.

Because few people are generalists, the one who is training needs to develop both the primary gifts of the person they are training but also needs to see what 'second strings' might be available so that a broader usage might be made of their giftings. For example, in a large church, someone might only be the leader of the music group. In a smaller church they might double as the leader of a fellowship group as well, even if leading a group is not their main gift area.

It takes a long time to develop leaders for the small church. There is also a strong possibility that the kind of leadership development that takes place will actually inspire those who are being trained to enter full time Christian ministry themselves. That is a great testimony to the minister in the small church, but it can also be intensely frustrating. One way of offsetting that kind of loss is to see whether it might not also be possible to persuade those who are in larger churches to come and benefit from the kind of relational training that takes place in the small church. Some people will prefer the slower pace of life and leadership in the small church. Admittedly, it takes time to win acceptance for such incomers, but it is not impossible to look outside the small church for willing volunteers.

The Place of Mission

The small church is a place where each one is known. The experience of being known and of knowing others is a positive benefit and one which is not always available outside of the small church. On a number of occaisions I have spoken to those who have acted as interim moderators (or the denominational equivalent) for small churches looking for clergy. These individuals have almost always come from larger churches. Their experience of working with small churches was a combination of wonder at the warmth of it all, and worry about the lack of awareness of the wider Christian world. The simple fact is that the small church often has very limited horizons.

Those kinds of limited horizons are neither necessary nor

helpful. In recent years, many small churches, especially those in the inner city, have been helped by the introduction of mission teams supplied by organisations such as Oasis, Youth for Christ and Youth With a Mission. A small team, usually of four young people, comes to work with the church for a year at very little cost to the church. These missionary efforts represent significant initiatives for many small churches which have been looking for leadership resources from outside of their own situation.

Mission is a two way process. Just as there have been many churches which have been helped by teams coming in, so it is also true that those small churches which have been willing to embrace an interest in missions have seen their horizons develop enormously. At one time the only realistic way for a small church to be involved in mission was to contribute a relatively small amount to the total support of a missionary programme or project. I have met a good number of missionaries who have been aware that their most faithful support has come from a network of small churches.

We now live in an ever shrinking world, a global village, as some have described it, and other possibilities for mission are now emerging. Perhaps the most exciting involvement that any church can have with the mission field is to take a team to another country for two or three weeks. A British small church that interacts with another small church in France, India, the Middle East or Ghana will never be the same again. Here is a context in which leadership skills will be developed rapidly and concepts which were difficult to communicate in a P.C.C. meeting become instantly understandable. A church that invites visitors from other lands and cultures to share with them for a time will almost certainly be changed by the experience. An awareness of the universality and diversity of the church around the world will help the small church to build its own community of faith more quickly and more dramatically than any other single factor. Smallness of size must never mean smallness of faith and vision. Mission involvement helps a congregation to be a small church with a large vision. Small churches which embrace mission help to develop the ecology of mission.

Notes

1. Carl S Dudley, *Making the Small Church Effective*, (Abingdon Press: 1978), p 62.
2. The tendency of the small church to resist leadership is also discussed in Chapter 9 of this book.
3. Carl S Dudley, *Making the Small Church Effective*. (Abingdon Press: 1978), p 62.
4. *Ibid*, p 66.
5. *Ibid*.
6. *Ibid*, p 68.
7. *Ibid*, p 49.
8. *Ibid*, p 56.
9. *Ibid*, p 56f.
10. For a fuller discussion of the place of giftedness in the small church see Chapter 14 of this book.

PART 3
Strategies for the Small Church

CHAPTER TWELVE

TAKING THE FIRST STEP

The contrast between the small church and the large church is similar to that between a family and a business. This is not to suggest that the large church is only a business anymore than the small church is only a family. But there is a clear difference in the way in which the life of the large and the small church is ordered. A business, by its very nature, finds it easy to to think in terms of the future, of plans and of strategy. A family, while it does make plans and does consider the future, is much more concerned with relationships than with strategies. For this reason, it is often much more difficult for the small church to know where to begin when considering issues of strategy. Such language is alien to who the small church is. It is hard to see through the fog of personal feelings. How then can we help the small church launch out on a journey that involves careful thought about the future?

Regardless of the length of the journey, it always begins with the first step. The first few steps can be critical ones. They initiate our basic direction in a situation where we might know the destination but almost nothing about the route that we should take. Not knowing what the first step should be can paralyse a church and produce either inaction or worse still inappropriate action. What follows are seven suggestions which, taken together, can help your church to determine its first step.

Philosophy of Ministry

When I first heard this phrase I was confused as to what it meant. Was it some kind of grand underlying set of presuppositions which determined the approach that one took to the whole of ministry? If so, I thought that would take me the remainder of my ministry to determine. To my relief, on further investigation I discovered that it was much simpler than that. The term comes from the field of church growth thinking and is often used by writers such as Peter Wagner, Eddie Gibbs and Roy Pointer. In essence, your philosophy of ministry is determined by the answer to the question, 'Why is this church here?'

For many churches, and especially small churches, the immediate response to a question such as this will often be to say something like, 'We are here, because we are here, because we are here'. In other words, as far as anyone can remember there has always been a church here and there hopefully always will be. Such a reply may well be true, but it is not very instructive in terms of helping a church to grapple with the question of its specific ministry or purpose in relation to the community that it seeks to serve.

The question 'why are we here?', is not a deep philosophical question about the purpose of life, so much as a pressing question about the contemporary relevance of a particular congregation. Such a question comes into much sharper focus when someone else, perhaps someone in the denominational hierarchy, suggests to us that there is no legitimate reason for our church to be in existence and that it would be much better if we closed the doors of the church forever. Such suggestions are not infrequently made to the members and leaders of small churches.

I always enjoy watching the television series, *The Trouble-shooters* in which the former chairman of I.C.I., Sir John Harvey Jones, seeks to help a variety of businesses and other institutions identify their problems, opportunities and potential strategies. When you have watched a number of episodes you begin to realise that no matter what the situation, there are certain key questions that the 'troubleshooter' always asks, The first and most basic question that is asked in all his cases is 'What business are you in today?' Not 'What business were you in or might you be in?' Not even 'What are all the things that you do?' although that becomes important later. The key issue is always that question which seeks to unearth the core activity or reason for being in business at all. We might also ask of each local church, 'What business are you in today?'

How does a church go about the task of answering such a question? In many cases the focus of a small church is the community in which it is set. What does a church want to accomplish for the community? 'Just being there', is not really sufficient as a response. It clearly cannot be the intention of the church to exist in order to provide an attractive architectural background to improve the appearance of the community, or just to be there in order to provide a better marriage and funeral service. So how do we describe the basic call that God has given us as a local church.?

The answers may be many and various. There will be some churches that have a clear community focus. There will be others who see themselves as having a specialist function within the community—fulfilling a role within the broader Christian community that no other church is meeting. There will also be a few churches who have a very different function. They might see their purpose as being intimately connected to the fact that they are the only church that represents a particular element of the broader Christian tradition within a given area. For example, they might be the only church with a baptistic tradition, or they might be the only church with a pentecostal position or a reformed doctrine. It might be style of worship or commitment to an ideal. Very often there will be more than one basic reason for the existence of a church. Whatever the reasons are, if the entire congregation is agreed as to why they exist as a church, it is helpful to know and to place it on record.

The result of this process can be written up and used as a mission statement. A mission statement completes the sentence that begins, 'This church exists to. . . .' It is very common for churches to have three or four focal points in such a statement. It is helpful if a church can produce a mission statement that is easy to remember. This can be accomplished by such simple techniques as using words that all begin with the same letter of the alphabet. For example, words like caring, community or communicate often feature in mission statements. Having produced a simple, clear statement, it needs to be used as often and as visibly as possible. It can go on the church headed paper, on the notice board, in the parish magazine, in every and all communications that the church sends out. It should be possible for every member in the church to remember the basic content of a good mission statement.

David Pitts, writing in the *Church Growth Digest*, suggests that mission statements should feature five criteria.[1] They should:

1. Be portable. People should be able to carry the statement in their memories.
2. Have direction. They should carry within them a suggestion as to the further action that should be taken to implement the mission statement.
3. Define what the organisation does. In other words be clear as to what basic business the organisation is in.
4. Make clear who the organisation exists for.
5. Articulate the manner in which the mission is to be conducted. The core values of the organisation should be reflected in the mission statement.

Purpose, Goals and Values

The philosophy of ministry process resulting in a mission statement effectively answers the question of purpose for a church. But that long term vision needs to be seen in creative partnership with two other vital ingredients. The first of these is goals. The words 'goal' and 'planning' are often viewed with some suspicion in the Christian community. The church growth writer Jim Montgomery, recognising this problem, readily admits that the process of goal setting can be a 'carnal activity'. He recognises that goal setting can induce many unhelpful attitudes such as pride and even a kind of competitive spirit. However, he also helpfully points out that the exercise of goal setting can be an intensely spiritual activity. He continues:

It can be an honest attempt to obey more effectively our Lord's command, to be a doer of the Word and not a hearer only.'[2]

The setting of goals can helpfully focus our attention on what it is that we want to accomplish in the next immediate period of time. Such a discussion helps us to assess what resources we might need in order to accomplish the goals we have set. In discussing the goals which we wish to agree there are two kinds of guidelines to consider.

First, it is tempting to set goals which are a long way in the future. To some degree, the further away a goal is, the less useful it is. We cannot really know what the future will hold, whether we will still be part of the congregation in ten years time; whether the needs of the church and the community will have changed, or even whether some unforeseen events will have made our goals look completely foolish. A very long term goal might almost be better expressed in terms of the purpose of the church rather than as a goal. Short term goals (twelve months), and medium term goals (three to five years), are much more useful.

The second temptation is to set goals which are so general in their scope that no-one will ever be able to tell whether or not we have achieved them. Roy Pointer in his book *How Do Churches Grow?* lists five characteristics of good goals.[3] He says that they should be:

— Relevant—related to accomplishing the goal.
— Measurable—allow us to know how and when we have accomplished the goal.
— Achievable—be within our resources to achieve.
— Significant—make a difference to our situation.
— Personal—involve those who are setting the goals in meeting the goals.

The one ingredient in the above list that gives churches the greatest difficulty is that of measurability. We are all too prone to set goals which are sufficiently vague that they cannot be measured. The stated goal, 'We want to start a work to reach men', at first glance looks very specific but on closer inspection turns out not to be so. What would constitute a men's work?; What would represent success? are just two immediate questions. The statement 'We want to start a work to reach men' needs a good deal of further refinement before it becomes a measurable goal.

Assuming that the church has been able to set a number of clear goals, it is also important to begin talking about the values that underlie the life of the church. It can be surprisingly easy to agree purpose and goals but then to have great difficulty agreeing the area of values. Yet it is essential to do so because failure to recognise and communicate values produces far more conflict than a failure to agree on purpose or goals.

Some years ago I was the minister of a church which had broadly agreed its purpose and its goals. These were not set out in formal statements but there had been a good amount of discussion as to the direction in which we were headed. Given that we had had such broad agreement I was constantly surprised by the degree of conflict that took place within the church, especially since we were progressing very well in terms of meeting our basic purpose and goals. I gradually came to realise that the problems we were having related to a clash of values. One of our goals had been to see people from the neighbourhood won to Christ. This was essential for a church where so many of the worshippers were commuting from the surrounding areas. However the more we succeeded, the worse the conflict became! The truth was that those who were coming into the church from the neighbourhood had a radically different set of values from those who were already in the church, and these different value systems had never been recognised or talked through.

Discovering the various values in a church is never easy, because they run so deep in who we are as people. Yet making the attempt to do so is vital. In order to draw out the values that people hold it is necessary to ask questions such as 'What does this church need to feel like in order for me to feel comfortable here?', or 'What is it about this church that is important to me?' Obtaining the answers to such questions is never easy. It usually takes much time but is always worthwhile.

Once a number of responses have been collected it will often become clear that the range of those responses is fairly diverse. Because God has made each of us different, some tend to be more task oriented, while others tend to be more people centred. There will be many other differences as well. The fact that there are differences does not matter so much as the fact that these differences are talked about, recognised and taken into account in the overall vision that the church has. This process is vital for any church regardless of its size but it is especially important for a small church because its single celled characteristic[4] means that it will be difficult to accommodate a number of emphases in the one church in the way that a large church can sometimes manage.

Strengths and Weaknesses

Some years ago, I came across some material from America which included the wonderful heading, 'A Church Growth Diagnostic Clinic'. Given my weakness for attractive terminology I turned with some expectation to the pages in question. Imagine my disappointment when what I found was only a means of assessing the strengths and weaknesses of a particular church. It didn't sound nearly as impressive when expressed in that way. But as the years have passed, I have found that simple approach to be one of the most effective tools for designing a strategy for a healthy church. Roy Pointer has a useful summary of such an approach in his book entitled, *The Growth Book* and a fuller account in *How Do Churches Grow*?[5] An outline of the same factors forms a unit in the Bible Society's Church Growth course.[6] Roy Pointer calls them 'Ten signs of a growing church'.[7]

How can one use such signs to evaluate a particular church? The value of such an approach lies entirely in their usefulness as self-evaluation on the part of church members themselves. I have used such outlines with many different churches and have been surprised to discover the high degree of unanimity in the perceptions of worshippers concerning their own church. Self-discovery by those who worship in a church is far better than a report brought by an outside expert. However, in view of the difficulty that the small church sometimes has in being objective about its own family life, it can sometimes be helpful for an outside person to act as a facilitator in order to enable the members of the small church to imagine how those outside the church might see them.

A useful way of conducting such an exercise is to spend an evening on the task with as many members as can be assembled. Each member needs a sheet of paper with the various categories listed and some kind of scoring against each one. This can be a scale of 1 to 6. (Not 1 to 5 otherwise there is a tendency to score 3 for everything). An even better approach is to use categories such as No Problem, Minor Problem, Major Problem, Serious Problem. The group leader needs to explain what is meant by each category so that there is a common agreement about what each 'sign of growth' means. Following this exercise it can be helpful to engage in group work to discuss the conclusions that the participants have arrived at.

Very clear patterns emerge from this kind of analysis. One can use an awareness of the strengths that are highlighted as the core ingredients in a future strategy. It is far better to build on strengths than to concentrate on rectifying weaknesses. One should not be too worried by the weaknesses that are identified. It is rarely possible to rectify every weakness in a church and it is usually foolish to try. True, there may be one or two areas that are so glaringly problematic that they cannot be ignored. But at least there will be a high degree of consensus about those factors. That then gives the leadership a head start in obtaining permission to introduce change.

Community and Church Audits

A second useful tool, which needs to be employed with the above analysis is one that has the same church growth origin, namely a Church and Community Audit. There are many such audits and each one has its own particular strengths. The Milton Keynes Christian Foundation,[8] has produced a useful publication entitled 'Mission Audit Pack'. In it you will find a wide range of audits and surveys to suit a variety of situations. At least one of them should meet the needs of your church.

The general rule with most of these survey tools is, the simpler the better! But even a simple audit is likely to lead to the well known church growth disease, 'Analysis Paralysis'. In the course of my travels I often come across churches who have engaged in a mission audit of one kind or another and then, having engaged in much hard work, have forgotten all about it. Why does this happen? Sometimes a church will put so much effort into an audit that it manages to give itself the impression that it is actually engaged in mission, when all it is really doing is obtaining the raw data with which to plan mission. Perhaps more frequently there is a real sense of puzzlement at how to use the material that has been collected. I occasionally encounter a church which has had the benefit of a computer expert in the congregation. Such a person has entered all the data onto a machine which has done all the number crunching and then has produced the information in the form of bar charts, pie charts, graphs and other assorted tables. Sometimes it is all beautifully presented in colour, with colour acetates as a bonus. But it is almost always the case that the more data that is presented, the harder it becomes to know what to do with it!

The key to overcoming such a situation is to interact with the information that is obtained by treating is as stimulus for prayer. 'What is God trying to say to us through this information?' is the most important question that we can ask. The likelihood is that asking such a question will result in other questions coming back to us. It may be that we need to obtain yet more information in order to answer these new questions, but the process of refining what we know through prayer will eventually lead us to concentrate on the very few specific areas that will be important for the future of our church.

Worship and Welcome

Robin Gamble in his book *The Irrelevant Church*[9] calls worship and welcome the 'bread and butter' of church life. The temptation for any small church is to imagine that because it is small, not nearly as much time needs to be spent on worship preparation. The very opposite is true. In some ways it is much more difficult for a small church to be able to provide a significant sense of warmth and well-being in worship than it is for a larger church, therefore it is all the more important to work hard at trying to accomplish it.

The two major ingredients in worship are usually those of music and the sermon. It can be very depressing to have eleven people, singing, 'O for a thousand tongues', especially when not all of them know the tune or could sing it if they did. When I have been in those situations I have been unsure whether we were offering a hymn of praise or uttering a prayer of intercession. If only God would send us just a few more worshippers, I would think to myself, I would settle for fifty tongues and leave aside the other nine hundred and fifty! Selecting the songs or hymns that work in a small group and finding musicians for a small church can be a major challenge.

The same temptation applies to preaching. It is hard work to preach effectively to a small church. To some extent the very medium of preaching lends itself to a larger congregation. It requires a different kind of skill to communicate with a smaller group of people. It may seem callous to say this in view of the dedication of those who preach in such situations, but very often smaller churches have not been served well by those who have been their preachers.

I recall preaching on a regular basis to a small church only to find that there was almost no interaction with the congregation. I could not seem to obtain any eye contact or indeed draw out any other response from them. After some weeks of this total non-reaction I was beginning to doubt my ability as a communicator, until one week I went to preach at another, larger church nearby. I used the same sermon from the previous week, one which had not received a very enthusiastic response from my regular small church. As you can imagine I went with some trepidation after my experience of the previous few weeks. To my amazement the congregation responded to my every word and heaped appreciative comments on me afterwards. It then began to dawn on me what had been happening. The small church that I had been serving had been so used to receiving some rather poor preaching stretching back over many years, that they had become accustomed to the idea that the sermon slot was the time to switch off, think about something else and just wait until it was all over. This reaction did not even seem to be a conscious one. It had simply developed slowly over a period of time until even the most hardy members of the flock had been mesmerised into a semi-conscious state. I won't tell you of my strategy for changing this state of affairs in case you are tempted to try it—suffice it to say it wasn't a good idea!

When it comes to the area of welcome, I have found that many small churches view themselves as being very welcoming places. One church that I know conducted an internal survey of their strengths. Although they were very perceptive in most areas they had real difficulty in assessing the degree to which they were a welcoming church. Almost every person had scored the church very highly in the area of welcome and as far as the members were concerned they were very warm and caring. However, as a visitor I found that the extent of their care for each other was so all absorbing that they did not always notice that it did not extend to their visitors. At the close of the benediction there seemed to be an enormous sideways rush as members warmly embraced each other and gathered in tight huddles leaving myself and one or two other very obvious visitors feeling slightly uncomfortable in the centre aisle. At least the visitors could welcome each other. They certainly all knew who the visitors were!

Obtaining a balance in this matter is extraordinarily difficult. It can be even worse to over-welcome the visitor. Anyone who visits a church that has less than the low thirties in attendance will almost certainly feel fairly exposed already and possibly only too anxious not to feel trapped by endless questions after the service. Identifying those who can be both welcoming and sensitive to the feelings of visitors will be important in getting the welcome right. Few people have such skills. Not only will an emphasis on worship and welcome encourage visitors to return, it will also greatly enhance the sense of well-being that the existing congregation has.

The Church Building

Most small churches occupy buildings which they have inherited from the past. That inevitably means that some buildings are not entirely appropriate for the church that is now using them. In the case of some churches the buildings are much too large for the church now meeting in them. Other churches have buildings that strongly reflect the age in which they were built and so do not seem to be suitable for ministry in contemporary culture. Even in cases where the building concerned is an ancient one and might be considered a real asset in terms of its beauty, its inheritance as a place of prayer over centuries, and as a building that induces a deep sense of worship, a problem can arise. The very strength of the building, namely its other-worldliness, seems to produce a sense of distance as secular people struggle to know how such a building can be part of their life, other than providing an attractive setting for baptisms, weddings and funerals.

Often the most difficult aspect of any older building, whether attractive or not, is the lack of suitable areas for activities other than worship. Midweek meetings, youth work and other demands which larger churches have as part of their programme, need to be accommodated in the buildings. In the case of those few small churches who do meet in modern buildings, there is often a multipurpose worship area which has to meet a large number of needs with all the attendant compromises that this entails.

As we suggested in Chapter 3, many small churches in inner city areas have rebuilt, redeveloped, or reordered the buildings in which they meet. Other types of small churches will have been able to engage in some modernisation of the building. But a more common difficulty for small churches is to be able to see the building as others see it. Buildings send out a powerful message to those in the community who never visit the church for any reason at all. Indeed, in the worst cases the building may even be a primary reason why many people never visit the church!

The first church in which I ministered was set in a small building but from the point of view of those of us who met there it was very attractive. Most of us commuted and a good number did so by car rather than by public transport. There was a good

car park which was surrounded by some chain link fencing
which clearly marked off the boundary between the church and
the adjoining open area of land. The members spent most of
their time at the church on the inside of the building which,
despite some problems with the electric heating, was comfortable
and attractive. A few months after my arrival we began some
door to door calling. We always introduced ourselves by saying
which church we came from. Imagine our surprise when some
people couldn't place the church that we were from. One man
in particular was puzzled. He lived a few yards away from the
church and bought his newspaper every day from a shop
opposite our church building. Eventually light dawned. 'Oh
that place! I thought that was an electricity substation!' The
idea that someone should have thought of our attractive modern
building in that way was something of a shock. Yet the more we
looked at it the more we understood what he meant. The notice
board could not be read by the majority of people who passed
the building and there was nothing else, not even a cross, to
indicate that the building was a church. Not long after this
discovery a number of changes, including the erection of a
cross, were implemented. Thinking hard about the outside of
the building and what it conveys through its notice board, the
immediate frontage of the church and the entrance area will
help us to see what those who are outsiders to the church
conclude long before they ever visit the inside of the church.

The inside of a building also matters. For those who have
attended a particular building for many years, familiarity dulls
the senses. Members of a small church do not attend in order
to admire the decor of the church but to meet their friends.
That sense of friendship and welcome within the group tends
to obscure the extent to which a person sees their surroundings.
In the first instance it will be these physical surroundings that
convey a sense of welcome or rejection to those who are
attending for the first time. Attention to the provision of toilets,
the general cleanliness of the building, and the care with which
it is repaired will speak loudly to those outside of the circle of
the small church who might be seeking to come inside that
circle. Why is it that we sometimes accept standards in our

church buildings that we would be very unlikely to accept in our own homes? What does that say to the newcomer in terms of welcome?

The same principles will be true for those small churches which meet in rented accomodation. In some ways they will have to work even harder than those who own their own building. The very fact of meeting in rented premises will sometimes mean that a credibility gap has been created. The smallness of the group might add to the problem. Working hard to help the sports hall, lounge bar, creche, or school classroom, feel and look more like a place of worship can help to overcome this credibility gap.[10]

Prayer

No church, whatever its size, can ever truly be a healthy church without a deep prayer life. It is even more true that no significant change is likely to take place in a church without a deep commitment to prayer. The gradual encouragement of a commitment to pray is important, not only to strengthen and sustain the life of a church, but also to begin the necessary process of change that many smaller churches need to make in order to rediscover their unique call from God. Prayer can often be a useful point of communication between those who would like to see change and those who are not so sure. It is a common language and it is a point of familiarity on which much else that is new can be built.

I never cease to be surprised about the extent to which people value prayer and engage in it. One survey, published in the book *British Social Attitudes*, suggests that around 16% of people in Britain attend a church service two or three times a month and that 27% of people in Britain pray at least weekly[11] Having said that people value prayer and claim to practise prayer, it is also clear that few people know much about prayer. This is not the place to give such instruction but some action points can be suggested.

First, identify those who already pray on a regular basis and utilise that resource by giving them regular items to add to their prayer concerns. Finding the natural intercessors in a church is one of the most strategic developments a church can engage in.

Secondly, provide practical teaching on prayer through the regular preaching and teaching of the church. Use the forum of small house groups where prayer may take place to tease out the practical questions that people who pray begin to uncover.

Thirdly, find natural points at which prayer can be encouraged in the existing life of the church. For example, I recently visited as a tourist a beautiful country church that had made an impressive effort to provide a rota of people to sit in the building and offer a welcome and information to those who like me, came to look round. The members of this church all gave one hour of their time on a Saturday. I noticed that some of those on the rota had brought knitting or other tasks to help them use the time when no visitors were present. It struck me at the time that the church might have been greatly helped if perhaps ten minutes of each of those hours had been given to prayer. That would not have involved any extra meetings or additional time commitment but it could make a huge difference to the life of any church.

Fourthly, work with the members of the church to agree long term prayer targets and shorter term intercessory needs. When people who are committed to pray discern God's answers the effect will be to increase the commitment to prayer.

Fifthly, ensure that there is continued feedback in terms of the progress that is made in relation to the matters that are being prayed for. These should be regularly communicated to the entire church by using the regular channels of communication both formal and informal.

Those who engage in such prayer will often become the catalysts for change in a church. Their prayers will help to identify the next step to take. Even when that step is clear, prayer will assist in providing wisdom in implementing the next step. Those who pray will be valuable allies in securing gradual and effective evolution as compared with the convulsions of an insensitive revolution. Those who are committed to pray are often more patient in progressing change than those who are committed to action alone.

All of these suggestions will help the small church to regain momentum in their journey of faith. It may be that only a few of these suggestions will prove to be necessary for a given church. Some churches might take only one ingredient and find that it provides a real breakthrough. In any case, as each step is taken and results are noted, faith increases ready for the next step of the journey.

NOTES

1. David Pitts, *Church Growth Digest*, Vol. 14 No. 2, pp 12ff.
2. Jim Montgomery and Donald McGavran, *The Discipling of a Nation*, (Overseas Crusade: 1980), p 130.
3. Roy Pointer, *How Do Churches Grow?*, (Marc Europe: 1984), p 171ff.
4. A discussion on the character of a small church as a single cell organisation can be found in Chapter 2.
5. Roy Pointer, *The Growth Book*, (Marc Europe: 1987), pp 26–33 and *How Do Churches Grow?*, *op cit*, pp 68–104
6. Bible Society Church Growth course information can be obtained by writing to the Society at Stonehill Green, Westlea, Swindon, SN5 7DG.
7. The Ten Signs of Growth which are displayed by growing churches are:
   — Constant Prayer
   — Respect for Biblical Authority
   — Effective leaders
   — Mobilised Membership
   — Eventful Worship
   — Continuous Evangelism
   — Community Life
   — Compassionate Service
   — Openness to Change
   — Released Resources
8. The Milton Keynes Christian Foundation can be contacted at 4 Church Street, Wolverton, Milton Keynes, MK12 5JM.
9. Robin Gamble, *The Irrelevant Church*, (Monarch: 1991).
10. M Robinson and S Christine, *Planting Tomorrow's Churches Today*, (Monarch: 1992), pp 276ff contains a longer discussion on how those churches which use rented premises can improve their appearance.
11. Jowell, Brook, Prior, Taylor (Eds.), *British Social Attitudes— the 9th Report*, (Dartmouth) p 56.

CHAPTER THIRTEEN

NETWORKING THE SMALL CHURCH

The relationship between the church in the town and the church in the countryside constitutes a very complex story throughout the history of the Christian faith. It has often been noted that Christianity began life as an urban faith, a factor which strongly influenced its early development.[1] The developed church in the larger town or city was rarely a small church in the first centuries of the Christian church. It was only later that the church in the town sought to expand its mission to win the countryside for the gospel. The churches that were established in villages and hamlets were necessarily different in style, size and ethos from the strong urban churches which characterised the early locus of Christianity.

How different the church looked in medieval England! Christianity was no longer primarily an urban faith, despite the importance and influence of the cathedrals and the city based churches. By the twelfth century a strong network of parishes covering the entire territory of England had become the dominant feature of church life. This development was a reflection of the relative financial importance of rural areas as compared to urban centres. Wealth, settlement, population and so political power was strongly oriented towards the countryside. This represented a sharp contrast both with Europe and England in Roman times when urban life had been so dominant.

The fact that the medieval church was so strongly oriented towards the countryside does not necessarily mean that the rural church was always a thriving concern. The book *Church and Religion in Rural England* makes the point that:

Following the medieval problems of reduced populations in the Black Death, of earlier absentee priests and of monastic and Papal interference, the parochial system was in need of a dedicated workforce. So it was that a distinctive feature of the English Reformation was a commitment to pastoral obligation at the parish level. . . The parish came to be the pragmatic focus of the English Reformation ideal. New vision and energy was brought to the pre-existing parochial structure of the land.'[2]

So powerful was this renewal of a rural ministry throughout the course of the Reformation that during the Victorian period it was church life in the countryside that was seen as the norm and as providing a living expression of the Christian faith. By contrast, the newly emerging cities and other urban areas were seen as essentially evil places where it would be difficult for the Christian faith to survive at all. Indeed one writer has credited the evangelical Clapham Sect as pioneering the creation of suburbia as a way of insulating family life from the evils of the city, where Christian men necessarily had to earn their living, but did not want their wives and children exposed to city vices. Suburbia, as a place where the ideals of rural life, with large gardens, fresh air and space, could be combined with the convenience of access to the city, was their preferred solution. If this analysis of the origins of suburbia is correct, it is hardly surprising that Christianity in the twentieth century has become so strongly identified with suburban life!

This brief sketch of the various self-understandings of the natural locus for the Christian faith is further complicated by the emergence of strong religious diversity as a consequence of the religious evangelical revivals of the late eighteenth and early nineteenth centuries. The greatest impact of the revival in terms of the number of new chapels tended to be in the newly emerging communities of the industrial revolution. With the exception of some rural areas where mining was important, such as Cornwall with its tin mines, the new Nonconformist denominations such as Methodism, increasingly saw their numerical strength as lying in the towns. Therefore the problem for the Nonconformists was how to use their strength in the towns to reach out to the countryside.

For the Anglicans who had little initial strength in the new towns, the problem was much more complex. The historian David Thompson, in a useful study of church extension in the nineteenth century, quotes from an Anglican bishop as follows:

> The significance of the countryside has been recognised by historians in so far as it was the former home of the many migrants to the towns, whose spiritual welfare constituted the major challenge of the age. This was also the contemporary view. But the reciprocal nature of even this relationship has not always been realised. Bishop Magee of Peterborough made this point in Leicester in 1869: 'This new population that comes in by so many hundreds and thousands a year, represents not only the successful labours of religion in the country, but all the evils and all the defects of country work. If there has been a neglected parish . . . and if there comes from that place an immigration into the town of Leicester . . . we must feel that the town of Leicester is deeply interested in the spiritual work of the county. And then as the inhabitants of the town return into the country villages, we ought both clergy and laity to feel interested in the spiritual condition of this town of Leicester. The whole blood of the diocese is ever circulating through this great town, and according to the condition of this heart of the county, will be the spiritual condition, more or less, of our country parishes.[3]

The truth was not that the countryside represented a great strength from which the new towns could be evangelised, so much as the whole task of evangelisation depended on a complex relationship between the two. As David Thompson also notes in the same study:

> But in many parts of the country rural evangelism was felt to be as urgent a priority as urban evangelism. The church of England sought to overcome the consequences of rural neglect; and all Nonconformists, not only Methodists, attempted to involve town members in the life of country chapels.[4]

This last quotation from Thompson gives a strong clue as to the nature of the strategy that was adopted by all of the denominations as a means of strengthening the work of evangelisation. In particular it refers to their attempt to assist the work of smaller churches whether in the town or the countryside.

A Co-operative Approach to Church Extension

Although organised on the basis of dioceses and further sub-divided into Archdeaconaries, the balance of power between local parishes and the diocese has often been such that the Church of England has not always acted as though it were a single ecclesiastical body in a given geographical area. Nevertheless, in the second half of the nineteenth century, there is a good deal of evidence that Anglicans did have cohesive plans for mutual co-operation and support. In practical terms that often meant that more help was available for church extension in the towns than in the country areas but this was not exclusively the case. Some country churches were built at the same time as town and city extension was taking place. But the essential point is not where the help was given, so much as the fact that there was an attempt to identify the areas of greater need, and in responding to that need, to work co-operatively across the diocese.

Similarly, in the case of denominations which had a stronger congregational basis, such as the Baptists and the Congregationalists, the second half of the nineteenth century witnessed a much stronger effort to draw on the potential strength of local associations in order to extend the work of the church in those areas where a particular denomination felt its witness to be weak. In practise, this often meant that Nonconformists were able to expand their work in the countryside. It also enabled them to open churches in towns and in the newer areas of the larger cities where no work would have been pioneered without a co-operative effort.

Perhaps the most interesting example is that of the two major Methodist denominations, the Primitives and the Wesleyans, whose circuit organisations provided a strong co-operative framework for church extension. The circuits of that time revealed a strikingly different pattern to that which prevails in Methodism today, some of which are entirely urban and others which are entirely rural. While it is also true that there remain many circuits that contain a mixture of suburban and rural congregations, or suburban and urban congregations, the overall pattern is nevertheless rather different from that which prevailed for much of the nineteenth century. At that time it was much more common for the circuit to provide an institutional link between town and country.

David Thompson points strongly to this connection between town and country in Methodism and views it as one of the most important factors in allowing Methodism to have a strong influence on village life. He quotes from a study of rural religion in Lincolnshire which claimed:

> Only through Methodism did the towns have much effect on village religious life . . . The circuit, the key unit of Methodist organisation, brought preachers and people from towns and villages into regular contact with each other and made it possible for the financial and human resources of the town chapels to contribute to the life of the outlying village chapels . . . it is an example of a situation where the money and men available in any one place were not sufficient to carry out what the church concerned wished to do there. It was therefore necessary to tap the resources of other places to help.[5]

Current church growth teaching indicates very clearly why such an approach to church life worked so well. It was not just a matter of the sharing of financial resources and of ministry, helpful as this was. What we see in the expanding circuit system of the nineteenth century was a classic example of the 'Cell, Congregation and Celebration' model propounded by church Growth thinkers.[6]

What does such a model teach us? The claim is that growing churches usually have three levels of organisation contained within them. The level of Cell, usually 6–10 people, is that of the small group, meeting together for mutual encouragement and support. The key word to describe the function of this group is 'Intimacy'. The Congregational sized group, normally between 25 and 70 people, is described by the key word 'Identity'. In other words this group has a uniting common factor which allows those who are in the group to feel that they belong to each other in some way. The common factor could be geographical location, or age group or a specific goal or task. The specific common thread is not important. All that matters is that those who are in the group recognise that there is a common factor and that they have a strong sense of what that factor might be.

The final category of Celebration refers to a group which is more than about 150 people. Once again the precise numbers are not as important as the function of the group which can be described by the word 'Inspiration'. We are probably all aware that something takes place in worship when a large group of people are gathered together that does not happen in smaller groups. This is not group hysteria. It is simply the case that the smaller the group the more aware we tend to be of our immediate surroundings while the larger the group the more anonymous we can be. A degree of anonymity can actually help us to concentrate on the divine.

One Anglican vicar who had spent most of his long ministry working with rural congregations told me of his decision to take nearly all of the regular attenders of his rural church, together with some others, to a large Billy Graham event. It was a decision that he had made after much hesitation. He was inclined to wonder about the relevance of a meeting in a large city centre comprising such a large crowd to a group of people whose normal worship service never exceeded a figure of a hundred, even on the most special of festival occasions. Yet he discovered that it was a very significant decision. He noticed that many of this flock were in tears during the hymn singing. He asked his folk later, 'Why did this event mean so much to you?' One man summed it up for all the others: 'We never knew there were so many Christians in the church of which we are a part.' There is something mystical and profoundly valuable about finding opportunities to express our belonging to the wider body of Christ.

How can we apply such insights to the Methodist circuit system? The base unit of the Methodist church of the previous century was that of the class. Every Methodist was required to be part of a class, or small group, in which a deeper spiritual life could be fostered. The class leader was a key figure in the lay leadership of the Methodist church. The various congregations, especially in the villages, acted as units which provided a geographical identity with the Methodist cause, while the circuit was seen as a unit which allowed the congregations to feel part of a greater whole. There might not have been an actual experience of celebratory worship at the circuit level, but there was certainly a sense of the celebration of a vision which came from an active involvement in the missionary enterprise of the circuit. In other words, the circuit provided a clear means by which every Methodist church in a given area could be networked with each other, for the benefit of all.

What has happened to such a system? Clearly, although the circuit still exists as an administrative unit, much of the missionary intent that lay behind the circuit structure has now disappeared. Observing Methodist church life today, especially in rural areas, one is left with a strong sense that the old networks have gradually broken down, leaving many small churches rather isolated and in existence only as long as one extended or dominant family is prepared to keep the doors open. Often those in such a family represent both the church's greatest strength and its greatest weakness. The church would close down without them but can't grow with them.

In such a situation, if classes meet at all it can be as infrequently as once a year—hardly an environment in which to encourage intimacy! The congregations have gradually become the dominant unit, which although they look to the circuit to provide certain functions, often look rather defensively at the circuit, believing that they need to fight for their own interests as a congregation, sometimes in opposition to the demands of circuit life. There does not often seem to be a sense that the circuit is the primary unit with local congregations as expressions of that same life. Indeed, to make matters worse, it is often the case that many local congregations have become so small that they are really no more than house groups which happen to meet in buildings. This arrangement brings all of the disadvantages of maintaining an often unsuitable building with none of the potential advantages of being a small, flexible and intimate cell group.

Such comments are not designed to single out Methodists for criticism, so much as to illustrate a general process that has also taken place among many other denominations. The co-operative vision of the previous century has largely broken down. It is only more obvious in Methodism because the networks were previously so strong.

Time for a New Start?

If the small church is ever to refocus its efforts away from maintenance and towards mission, the re-creation of networks will be essential. Networking represents a powerful tool for resourcing much that a small local church can never accomplish on its own. For example, an area of great difficulty for most, if not all, small churches is that of youth work. Even if a small church does have some teenagers in their church, it is very unlikely that there would be sufficient numbers to form anything more than a cell group. A cell group will generally be insufficient to provide teenagers with a strong sense of identity with a given local church. However, if a number of smaller churches could network in such a way that their young people could have a larger group, or congregation, to use the term that we have worked with earlier, then there is a much stronger possibility of fostering their faith through to adulthood.

Recently, I visited one such experiment among a number of churches in Norwich. What did it look like? The following account briefly describes what I found:

The temperature in the church was colder than I liked. We stood in a circle, a group of workers praying for the service that was about to take place. The traditional church building was arranged in a way that was different from its usual layout. Screens stood in front of the altar. They depicted a scene from a living room. Some easy chairs and other simple pieces of furniture served to complete the effect. Chairs had been cleared from a large part of the regular seating area, leaving only some pews that started half way down the church. Loudspeakers at the front and a mixing desk at the rear of the church added to the sense that something different was about to take place. Within half an hour the church was largely full with around 150 young people sharing in a very contemporary celebration of their Christian faith.

The young people who attended this regular celebration came from a variety of churches in the city and from none. Some were new converts others were rediscovering their faith. It was clear that this event represented a lifeline of hope for many. In the past few months I have become aware of a good number of events for young people which although not exactly the same in form and content as the one that I had attended in this one location, represent something of a departure for work among young people.

Over the last twenty years, in fact since I was a teenager myself, I can remember various attempts by local churches to work together in the area of youth work. Many of these attempts foundered because the churches concerned found it very difficult to fully trust each other. All too often the question that arose was, 'If young people come to Christ through this work, which church will they go to?' Just as often, there was another question which was rarely if ever articulated. It went something like, 'If we encourage our few young people to go to this event, will we lose them to the church in this project which appears to have the largest young people's group?'. Sadly, the consequence of this lack of trust has been that every church lost many of their young people because no single church could operate a successful youth programme. Even more sadly, the failure to co-operate meant that there were usually no young people won to Christ for anyone to worry about where they might end up.[7]

The new co-operative ventures among young people that are beginning to emerge have often been stimulated by what we sometimes call para-church agencies. However, their work would not be possible without the growing willingness of churches to experiment in an area littered with past failures. Such developments are clearly encouraging. Certainly they do leave open some very big questions. Not, 'Which church will have the converts?', so much as 'Will these projects lead to the creation of youth churches? And if so, what is their long term future?' For the moment though, it is important that young people are reached for Christ even if no-one has found solutions to the difficult issues raised by these new forms of the church.

Youth work represents only one area of activity which can function better when churches learn to network locally with other churches. Is it possible for significant local networks to emerge? I want to point to three recent examples, one Anglican one Baptist and one which is largely Brethren in its origins, which offer some local models of networking as an indication of what can take place.

What better place to start than Camelot! Writing in *Anglicans for Renewal* magazine, Josephine Bax describes the creation of a process of networking among a rural group of churches known as the Camelot Group of parishes. The congregation of which she is a part is not just small but tiny! She points out that this is because the village in which the church is set has just over one hundred residents. Josephine writes:

> We are a tiny congregation—you can't play the numbers game here, although attendances have gone up recently. It is a happy one which works well together—we don't dread PCC meetings here. We come from every walk of life, and everyone pulls their weight to keep the church going, as indeed they need to in such a small outfit. I have to double as churchwarden and organist. There is the usual divide between traditionalists who only come to the 1662 services, and renewalists who come to the more modern form. Our treasurer, a Lt. Colonel, refuses to pick up the Mission Praise hymn book and puts a special thank-offering in the offertory box when we don't have a hymn from Mission Praise![8]

The Camelot group consists of eight such parish churches and is jointly served by a Team Rector and Team Vicar, helped by a band of retired clergy and lay readers. Nothing too remarkable in that arrangement, you might think, and you would be right. However the team context has provided a very conducive framework for the creation of a pattern of ministry networking which certainly is unusual.

The heart of what they have done is to use the structure of the five fold ministry pattern described in Ephesians, namely Apostles, Prophets, Evangelists, Teachers and Pastors, to help identify the various ministry gifts in all of the eight congregations regardless of whether the people concerned were ordained or lay. Having identified the people with those specific gifts, they have then used them as a single team to minister across the group.

Part of the concern that motivated this change of ministry pattern was that of manpower shortages. (Josephine points out in her article that in her diocese it is likely that the present 262 clergy will be down to somewhere between 130 and 140 clergy by the year 2,000.) But the effect of involving lay people in the team on a gift basis has not just been to solve a person power crisis so much as to bring a wider spiritual renewal to individuals across the eight parishes. The adoption of this pattern has helped to change an arrangement which felt like a mere administrative convenience, namely a practical response to the shortage of clergy, into a sense that this is really one church, bound together by ministry but expressing its life in each of the villages by means of the various parish church buildings. So the evangelistic gifts which two lay people seemed to demonstrate, were no longer to be used (or under used) within the context of a single parish church but could be used across all the eight churches. The same was true for two other individuals who displayed prophetic gifts. At the same time, the Team Rector and Team Vicar no longer had to be all things to every church in their care. The importance of this fundamental shift to a more strongly networked structure is that it has helped to move the Camelot Group from a pastoral and maintenance mode to a more mission mobilised stance.

The second and very different example is that of a group of three Baptist Churches in Cambridgeshire. In 1992, the Baptist Times reported that the 'Cambridgeshire Baptist Association has invested its entire financial resources—some £6000—in an imaginative bid by three of the county's village churches to establish a new ministry to encourage growth.'[9] The three churches referred to consist of one larger Baptist church with its own minister and two small Baptist churches which have combined their resources to enable a second minister to work mainly with the two smaller churches. One of the small churches concerned is located in a village, and the other in what was a village, but is now part of the overspill of suburban Cambridge.

Two features of this scheme, which at the time of writing is still only a proposal, are worth noting. First, it clearly is not a common scheme since the Association in question has spent all of its available resources on facilitating this one proposal! Secondly, not only is it unusual as a proposal within Cambridgeshire, it has taken a long time to come to fruition. The minister of the larger Baptist church in Histon has been at his present church for some 16 years and during that time has attempted to help a number of smaller churches. Some of those that he has tried to help in the past have closed down and others have indicated that they did not want continued help. Clearly the building of sufficient trust to allow networking to take place can take a long time to develop.

A third example of networking at a local level has slowly developed over the last few years among a number of congregations described as mostly 'interdependent free churches' in the general Bristol area. The co-ordinator of this network is Rob Scott-Cook, a minister in one of the churches in the group. Approximately 15 churches with 10–12 full time workers co-operate together in this venture. The largest church is around 200 strong and the smallest 12. A typical church in the network has about 50 people in attendance.

The vision that lies at the centre of this initiative is a view of the church that sees the need for Celebration, Congregation and Cell groups working together to strengthen the church. By working together to help facilitate all three of these expressions of the church, the congregations involved in this network believe that they can not only enhance their own life as congregations but extend the Christian witness that each congregation offers.

The level of Celebration is provided for by means of a monthly Celebration meeting which draws together the members of the churches in the network for a Sunday evening of worship which includes some evangelistic content. The network has experienced something of an increased momentum during 1993 which has resulted in them locating the Celebration meetings in a larger venue, a secular media facility known as the Watershed building in central Bristol. This location has the advantage of being attractive and well known in Bristol. Its somewhat neutral status helps to encourage those who attend to invite friends and other contacts to the meetings. Although the intention of these meetings is not exclusively evangelistic, a number of people have made decisions to become Christians in this context. At the time of writing, some 300 people attend these Celebrations.

The focus of the network is to provide meaningful and viable expressions of the church for local communities in Bristol through the congregations in the network. Some church planting has taken place and more is planned. The conviction of the network is that church planting can take place more effectively through co-operative effort. The workers in the churches meet together every two weeks for what is described as a team meeting. The informal agenda of these meetings provides encouragement, support and prayer for the network and its workers.

Although the expression at Cell level is in the care of each congregation, the training that takes place through the network enhances the activity of each local church. A monthly newsletter is produced which is distributed to those who attend the monthly Celebration. The whole enterprise is financed by means of an offering which again takes place at the joint Celebration. This very simple network, or 'fellowship of fellowships' as it has been described,[10] is very simple to operate but is sufficiently effective that enquiries have come from a number of other churches who have expressed interest in becoming part of the Avon Celebration, as it is also sometimes known.

Successful Networking

Networking offers a creative possibility for the future of many small churches. Gerald Coates has made the observation that even among the generally growing house church movement, it tends to be the churches which are strongly related to a network of other churches which are growing. Many of those which have no wider relationships are more often than not static. However, networking does not offer an automatic 'cure all' for every situation. I want to suggest that for networking to be successful at least the following four conditions also need to be present.

First, the churches which desire to network with each other need to be convinced that there is more to the church than the local church alone. This is not just a pragmatic consideration. It is important to have a view of the church which sees clearly that the church consists of the communion of saints everywhere which although it necessarily has a local expression is not limited to a particular local expression. What is implied in such a view is that it contains a growing recognition of the catholicity, or universality, of the church. Such a sense of the wider church allows a number of local churches to give sufficient priority to the network of which they are a part to enable it to function properly.

This does not mean that a particular network represents the entire catholicity of the church, but it does enable a local church to give some expression to participation in the wider communion of the church. A vision of catholicity helps to balance local traditions with the wider tradition of the church and thus enables the church to be both contextualised without becoming trapped by the very contextualisation which inevitably only works well for one time and one place.

Secondly, it is vital for churches to recognise that the nature of their relationship with each other is founded in ministry and not in administration. The puritan divine, Richard Hooker, who did so much to help the Church of England recognise the importance of the local parish and its ministry, also saw clearly that the heart of ministry belongs to the whole church. As the book *Church and Religion in Rural England* puts it:

> The minister was not created by an eclectic congregation even though he was set to serve a particular group of people. He was always a minister of the wider church who happened to serve in a particular place.[11]

A recognition of the five ministry gifts of apostle (one who pioneers new developments), prophet (one who hears God's word for a given situation), evangelist (one who is able to clearly communicate the gospel message), pastor (one who understands the needs of the flock) and teacher, (one who is able to explain the ongoing application of the Christian message), is the lifeblood of the relationship between a network of local churches. Those with apostolic, prophetic and evangelistic gifts may tend to be used beyond the local church and may even be used beyond a particular network as well. Those with pastoral and teaching gifts will often be used more locally, but even these ministries belong to the whole church and never entirely to one local congregation.

Thirdly, a network of churches needs to learn to move from issues of maintenance to issues of mission. A mission oriented church will cease to see the church as existing primarily for those who already come, and will begin to see the church as existing mainly, even if not entirely, for those who have not yet attended.

Fourthly, a network of churches needs to be able to recognise lay ministry and see it fully integrated into a team relationship with those who are called to be full time in the ministry. Not only will such an arrangement allow the church to draw on gifts which it would otherwise not have access to, it will also allow congregations to celebrate what it means to be the people of God, or *laos*, together. Ministry belongs to the whole people of God: it is not the exclusive preserve of an elite.

Networks of churches, consisting of both large and small congregations, which put into practise these four principles will enable all of the churches that they encompass, regardless of size, to be truly healthy churches.

As I dream of such networks of healthy churches, I remember the story of one lifelong member of a small church who used to pray a very unusual prayer. She would sometimes pray for a power cut, something which did happen occasionally in the countryside where she lived. A power cut meant that the congregation in her parish church would abandon the regular service in the large, cold and ancient parish church, a building where each had their own familiar seat, often far removed from others in the congregation. They would go instead to a room in a nearby large house, which was heated and lit by other means. There in that place they would sit in close relationship to each other and would often experience a depth of fellowship and worship which was absent at other times. For this spiritually adventurous lady, the highlight of the year was when the Deanery came together for their 'annual sing' as she called it. It was only at these times that she felt truly part of a body which she recognised as the communion of saints. Hopefully, the emergence of churches which belong to significant networks will reduce the need for such prayers!

Notes

1. A number of people have written on this theme in recent years. A useful exposition of the place of the city in the history of God's dealing with his people can be found in Raymond Bakke, *The Urban Christian*, (Marc Europe: 1987). See especially Chapter Four.

2. David, Watkins and Winter, *Church and Religion in Rural England*, (T & T Clark: 1991), p 12.

3. David Thompson, *Church extension in town and countryside in later nineteenth century Leicestershire*, a chapter in Derek Baker (Ed.), *The Church in Town and Countryside*, (Basil Blackwell: 1979), p 428.

4. *Ibid*, p 427.

5. *Ibid*

6. For further reflection on the Cell, Congregation and Celebration principle, see Peter Wagner, *Leading Your Church to Growth*, (Marc Europe: 1984), pp 206ff. See also Chapter 15 of this book.

7. Martin Robinson, 'The Emerging Church', *Church Growth Digest*, Vol, 14, No 2, p 17.

8. Josephine Bax, *Anglicans for Renewal*, Vol 50, p 4.

9. *Baptist Times*, 31st December, 1992: p 10.

10. Rob Scott-Cook offered this description to the author in a telephone conversation, 20 July 1993.

11. David, Watkins and Winter, *Church and Religion in Rural England*, (T & T Clark: 1991), p 13.

CHAPTER FOURTEEN

GIFTEDNESS AND GROWTH

The minister of one small church that I know spoke to me of his frustration. 'In this church there seems to be two kinds of people—those who are so overworked they are ready to burn out and those who are so underworked they are positively bored. Why can't we share out the work more evenly?', he wanted to know. This is not an unusual situation for the small church.

I sometimes hear people using the phrase in small churches, 'If you want something doing, ask a busy person!' As an observation of how a small church works this is very accurate. There tends to be a very small number of people, sometimes only one person, who are highly competent, committed and motivated. Those in a small church have come to know that if you want something done, and if one of those already competent but busy people agrees to do it, then you can be confident that it will happen. This is a very adequate strategy for keeping the life of the church functioning. One competent though busy person will be able to handle enough of the tasks in a small church to ensure that the doors open each week and that the essentials have been accomplished.

While this is a good strategy for short term survival, it hardly looks like the church of the New Testament which emphasises so strongly the ministry of every member of the body of Christ. We can't argue that such a pattern really allows every member of a small church to discover who they are in Christ and fulfil their true potential. Yet it is very rarely the case that a high proportion of members in a small church are really functioning in the areas in which they are gifted. There can be a large combination of factors at work in producing such scenario.

1. A limited number of volunteers

It is simply the case that there are a certain number of jobs that need doing in any church and in a small church there are far fewer people to do them. The very basic practical tasks in a church, such as playing the organ, leading the worship, cleaning the building, ensuring that the heating is functioning and so on, do not significantly increase in number just because a church is larger. The impact of having far fewer people to perform these basic tasks tends to mean that there is far less probability of there being a person in the church who feels called to perform each of these tasks. Instead, those in the church who are willing to work need to attend to the essential tasks just to keep the doors open. The result is that a few people, (or even just one person), perform these tasks, not because they feel called to do so, but because their level of commitment, or in this case, sense of duty, is sufficiently high that they will do these tasks whether they feel called to do them or not.

2. Finding a way in

A small church can easily become so dependent on those who are willing to do these tasks that the church becomes increasingly identified with that one person or small group of persons. Others begin to note that the church belongs in some important sense to that one serving circle. It is this kind of scenario that can lead to the already mentioned syndrome, 'can't stay open without them, can't grow with them'.

Willingness to serve becomes domination of a situation. That kind of domination prevents others from discovering the areas of their own potential contribution. Not only are the existing avenues of service already covered, but the very model in which service is offered become so inflexible that other more flexible models tend not to be considered. The scope for service tends to be limited only to those tasks which enable the church to function on a week by week basis. The potential gifts of others can be overlooked if they do not relate directly to the regular and essential functioning of the church.

3. The principle of equality

In many small churches the principle of equality has a very high priority. All are equal in the small church. Such a view does have a very sound basis in Christian thinking. However, there is a tendency to interpret the view that all are equal in God's eyes as meaning that all are the same in God's eyes. In other words, even in those small churches where there is a greater level of involvement than just the one or two faithful few, the approach tends to be that of the rota, regardless of gifts. If the church needs cleaning and cannot afford to pay a cleaner then there will be a cleaning rota and so on.

Such an approach to the principle of mutual ministry tends not to induce great joy among the participants. While it can produce a higher level of involvement of the members of the body of Christ than when the church is dominated by a few, that involvement is not well focused. Instead of using the Apostle Paul's analogy that each person's gifts represent a different part of the body,[1] the rota approach, if carried too far, suggests that at times everyone in the church is a hand, and at other times, everyone is a foot or an arm. In such a situation, the jobs get done but mediocrity not excellence tends to prevail. As Lesslie Newbigin puts it:

> . . . a Christian congregation must recognise that God gives different gifts to different members of the body, and calls them to different kinds of service. St. Paul's letters contain many eloquent expositions of this fact. Yet there is a persistent tendency to deny this and to look for a uniform style of Christian discipleship . . . The ear should not demand that the whole body be ears, nor the eye that all should be eyes. A bagful of eyes is not a body. Only when a congregation can accept and rejoice in the diversity of gifts, and when members can rejoice in gifts which others have been given, can the whole body function as Christ's royal priesthood in the world.[2]

Even worse, many who do possess a high level of giftedness in one area can find themselves serving in areas where they are clearly not gifted with the result that their willing service simply attracts criticism. I have on occasion met people who are highly gifted but whose misdirected service has resulted in such high levels of criticism that they have lost all confidence in their ability to serve in any area, including those avenues where they clearly do have a great deal to offer. No small church can really afford to treat their best assets in this way and yet they frequently do.

4. Liberating leaders

The small church tends to attract certain types of people. One of the characteristics of those in a small church is that many are hurt people who are looking for care. It may well be that a good number of those who attend will not contribute significantly at a leadership level. That will not be their gifting. But it is nevertheless true that one of the functions of good leaders is to help others discover and apply their giftedness. Therefore it is essential to have some good leaders if all are to find their gift and place in the church. But the small church often struggles to locate and liberate those in the church who do have a leadership gift.

One church leader recently described the leadership potential of his church to me in these terms. 'Some of my best people are disabled because they are still recovering from hurts received elsewhere. Others are new Christians and are not yet ready to serve with maturity. A few are limited in what they can give because they do not have Christian partners. Some are very gifted and have few debilitating problems, but are highly committed to their jobs which leaves them with very little time to give to the church.'

From his perspective, his small church had great potential, but really could not begin to explore much of what could happen because it had become a 'resting place' for those who really did have creative leadership ability, but who for a variety of reasons were not able to contribute that which they had. Enough church leaders have told me similar stories to convince me that this is not an unusual scenario. In such situations it will be those who are available, regardless of their giftedness, who will lead and serve.

Discovering Giftedness—A Hard Way to do Church

Those who are fortunate enough to have discovered their gift area and been given an opportunity, whether in church or at work, or in some other arena, to express that gift, will know what joy can flow from such a combination. But the joy comes at the end of such a process and rarely at the beginning. This inevitably means that although operating on the basis of giftedness is a great way to do church for those who are already doing it, it is a very hard way to do church for those congregations who have not yet begun. It is as well to be absolutely realistic about the pitfalls which might lie ahead for churches who want to explore giftedness as a way of doing church. Five factors make it especially painful.

A change of culture

It is one thing to make changes in a church but still keep the same basic framework and culture. It is quite another matter to make the kind of changes which are so fundamental that the very culture of the church is changed. Most churches can cope with the first, especially if they can see immediate benefits flowing from that change. It takes a much stronger leadership to help a church undergo a major culture change, especially when the supposed benefits from making such a change seem to be a long time coming. From the perspective of many in the pew, a major change of culture seems merely to be an unnecessary disruption of life as they know it. The members of the small church will often prefer a 'quick fix' solution designed to meet the immediate problem, rather than go down the much more demanding route of changing the culture of the church.

The time it takes

Working with people to help them discover where they are gifted and how those gifts might be applied is a very time consuming process. Not only does it take a long time for each individual to work through such a process for themselves, it also requires the input of a great deal of personal one on one contact time for the key leaders in a situation. Inevitably if the key leader(s) in a situation are using a high percentage of their time investing in such a process, other areas in the life of the church may well have to take a back seat for a while. That may be frustrating for many in the church, including the key leader(s)!

Who is gifted to discover giftedness?

Perhaps even more difficult than the investment of time, is the issue of whether the key leader(s) in a given church are themselves gifted and skilled in such a way that they are able to carry through such a process. It may well be the case that some in the church will need to be trained, or at least take advice in how to conduct a process of gift discovery. Those who are trained may well not be those who occupy positions of leadership. Alternatively it may be necessary to seek such expertise from outside of the church. In any or all of these situations there is an implied threat to, or judgment of, the existing leadership which will need to be very carefully worked through.

The mismatch of position and gifting

Although it may come as a painful realisation, in fact very few churches appoint people to leadership positions solely on the basis of their character and giftedness. It is much more common to ask three other questions, (although these questions are rarely articulated). First, how long has someone been a member? Secondly, which family group are they a part of? (A supplementary question here might be, which family group is in effect sponsoring them?). Thirdly, who will be offended if they are not appointed?

The question of how able a person is to do the particular job to which they are being appointed tends to be viewed as a rather secondary matter. This is even more so when the appointment is to a leadership role, rather than to a more obviously task oriented position. Thus when someone is asked to be an elder, while there may be some questions relating to their character, there are far fewer questions relating to their gift areas. Whereas when someone is being asked to act as a secretary then questions regarding their ability to type etc. tend to have a higher profile than questions of character. But in neither case is the much deeper question asked, 'How is this person motivated and how will this job allow their gift areas to be matched to their motivation?'

Not everyone will fit

Having gone through the long and sometimes difficult process of helping someone to discover their gift areas and motivation, the conclusion can sometimes be that there is no outlet in the church for their particular gifts. It is very hard for a small church to have to come to the conclusion that a member might need to look outside of the local church in order to fulfil their ministry, but it may just be true! That doesn't mean that they necessarily have to leave the church and find another church which can use them. It might mean working with a community organisation, or with a para church group, and the local church might well derive enormous benefit from contact with other agencies. For example, one church I know had a member who began to work for a Christian agency. It didn't take long for meetings to be punctuated with 'I know someone who can . . .' Nearly all of those new contacts came about as a result of involvement with a new network of resources made through the workplace. But on some occasions it may well be that an individual does have to move to another church, perhaps even a much larger one, in order to find a creative opening that will enable them to flourish and blossom.

Since all of this seems to be so painful, it is understandable if people are inclined to ask, 'is it worth it?' But let's just remember for a moment the description offered above by a church leader of his potential leaders. There is a far greater possibility of those who have been hurt receiving healing by being in touch with their gift areas. New Christians will often grow more quickly when they are operating in their areas of giftedness. A church which is sufficiently creative to utilise people's real giftedness will often look a much more attractive place to the non-Christian partner than the church which does not do so. Those who are so motivated by their jobs might well look twice at their church commitments, or lack of them, if some of the same gift areas that are so motivating at work can be offered to them in the context of the Christian community. The potential for this very different way of doing church is enormous.

What Exactly is Giftedness?

So far we have talked a great deal about giftedness without really describing what we mean by such a term. Christians sometimes debate the difference between spiritual gifts and natural talents. Often such debates produce more heat than light! On the one hand there are some Christians who see spiritual gifts as entirely unconnected to any natural abilities. On the other hand there are some who see spiritual gifts as identical to natural abilities. The theologian Arnold Bittlinger has attempted to take account of these contentious issues in a definition of spiritual gifts or charisms as he calls them:

> A charism is a gratuitous manifestation (or undeserved free offering) of the Holy Spirit, working in and through, but going beyond, the believer's natural ability for the common good of the people of God.[3]

Bittlinger's rather technical definition is attempting to convey the simple fact that behind every gift lies the creative, empowering hand of God. It is God who has made us and therefore, in an ultimate sense, every gift that a person displays comes from him. But it is important to remember that God has made us as a unique creation and not just as an empty repository for the purpose of adding in a few gifts so that we can function more effectively. Our giftedness is an intrinsic part of who we are as created beings.

The Christian organisation SIMA has pioneered work in this field.[4] Their research has been based on the conviction that every single person is an absolutely unique creation of God. It follows from this conviction that every person is also uniquely gifted in the sense that no one has exactly the same pattern of gifts and abilities as anyone else. There may be some strong similarities between people, but no two people are exactly the same. This insight is tremendously important because a more simplistic approach to gift analysis tends to produce the assumption that generally speaking everyone with the same gifts will be able to function in much the same kind of way. The reality is very different!

Even more critical is the insight that there is a very complex relationship between motivation and giftedness. SIMA maintains that there are five critical areas of activity which interact with each other in such a way that the content of each area produces an infinite number of variables. Although it would not be appropriate in the context of this book to explain the SIMA programme in detail, (that would require a book by itself), it is worth just mentioning the five areas that SIMA has identified.[5] First they ask the question, on a continuum that ranges from the abstract to the concrete, what combination of subject matter, or raw data, does an individual prefer to work with, ideas or practical constructs? Secondly, what are the circumstances or situations which cause a person to be motivated? Thirdly, what particular abilities does a person have so that no matter how many times they use them they never get bored? Fourthly, in what ways does a person choose to relate to others in a work situation? Fifthly, what end result always causes a person to be deeply satisfied?

Not only is it important to begin to recognise the unique patterns of giftedness in what SIMA calls each person's 'motivational pattern', it will also be essential to begin to consider how these various areas will fit together in a team situation. Failure to recognise what motivates each person in a team can easily lead to a misreading of other team members, or even to a complete breakdown of communication within a given team.

Given the complexity of this issue it would be tempting to conclude that this really is such a hard way to do church that it would be better not to try at all, or at least to wait until the church is wealthy enough to call in a professional consultant. For the small church this would be a long wait indeed! It is perhaps more important to call for sensitivity than for years of training. Patience and care can bring insight without the need for a consultant's level of expertise, valuable as this might be. In fact it is possible to make some real strides in gift discovery and so of mutual understanding at a very simple level.

How Do We Discover Our Giftedness?

There are many gift discovery exercises available.[6] Clearly some of these approaches will be more appropriate than others for particular settings. But what nearly all helpful gift discovery programmes have in common is a combination of helping people to have some idea of what we mean when we speak about gifts, together with an observation of how people actually behave. Let me describe one actual application of such a process.

Some years ago the house groups in our church began to explore the issue of spiritual gifts. The group of which I was a part had eight participants. First of all we began to study the various passages of Scripture that dealt with spiritual gifts. We soon realised that the Bible lists a great number of gifts and few people in the group were sure that they knew what all of these gifts were. After we had spent some time describing and discussing these gifts we tackled the thorny question 'Are there gifts which are not mentioned in the Bible?' We soon saw that the Bible itself never makes the claim that there are not!

The next step was to begin thinking about the gifts that each of us in the group thought that we had. We were each asked to pray and reflect on our own giftedness and to come back the next week with some ideas as to the kind of gifts that we thought we had. At the same time we were asked to go through the same process for others in the group. When we came together, we began to share, one by one, first of all the gift that we thought we had and then to listen to the gifts that others thought we had. What a night! It was glorious. There was such an amazing degree of unanimity, insight and affirmation that some in the group were almost shedding tears of joy. Our group experienced a tremendous amount of bonding in fellowship on that occasion.

However, there were still two more steps to go. First, there was a difficulty. We had to admit that there were some in the group for whom this first exercise was not enough. Their giftedness needed some further teasing out and we realised that this would require help from other leaders in the church. Secondly, we needed help with the process of finding outlets or avenues for service in which these gifts could be exercised. Clearly we needed the active co-operation of leaders in the church in the process of gift deployment. Both these steps pointed to the fact that most of us in the group would benefit from some training,—not to train us to use gifts that we didn't recognise, but to allow us to enhance and derive the greatest benefit from the gifts that we already had.

In working through this process there were a few simple but

critical ground rules. First, no-one was allowed to comment on
the gifts that they thought others didn't have. We did not allow
any sentence that began 'I don't think that you have the gift of
. . .' Each contribution needed to be a positive one. Secondly,
the leader of the group ensured that before the evening began
they were able to identify at least some gifts in each group member. In the occasional case where they had difficulty, they con-
sulted with other leaders in the church. Thirdly, the process of gift
deployment, together with the implications of that for the church,
were considered by the leadership of the church before the
groups reached the stage of actually identifying each other's gifts.

How Do We Utilise Gifts in the Service of the Church?

There are some real dangers inherent in gift discovery exercises, given the context of a society where values are very much
oriented around consumerism and the 'me, myself and I' generation. Such values give rise to the tendency for some to see the
reason for the existence of the church as providing a platform
for their gifts and ministry, rather than seeing their gifts and
ministry as a means of benefitting the life of the church.

The background for the discovery and deployment of gifts in
the church needs to be one of sound discipleship. Many church
leaders complain that they simply cannot mobilise their members.
Often they will say that this is their primary problem since it
is almost impossible to implement ideas without people to
operate the programmes. The hard truth is that you cannot
mobilise believers, you can only mobilise disciples. Very few
churches have good discipleship programmes in place for their
new members. Most churches work on the discipleship by
osmosis theory, which suggests that if new members hear
enough sermons, sit on enough seats, attend enough meetings
and are around other members for long enough, then they
will just pick up what it means to be a Christian. Although
one could make a case for discipleship by osmosis in an
entirely Christian culture, what new believers actually pick up
without thorough discipleship training are the values of our
secular culture, many of which are completely antithetical to
Christianity. Although it may not be possible to disciple every

member before beginning a process of gift discovery, it is important to have a clear idea of the servant values inherent in discipleship, so that these can be clearly taught in parallel with the gift discovery process.

Be aware that gift identification will not necessarily lead to gift deployment unless it is matched with other factors that will help to motivate the individual concerned. The fact that someone has a gift does not mean they will use it even after they have become aware of it. For example, it may well be that a person has all the gifts needed to work with young people. And it may also be that your church urgently needs someone in this area. It does not follow that someone who has these gifts will be motivated to use them in this way. There may well be other factors in their personal make-up that would cause them to come alive in a completely different environment.

It is possible to draw up a list of openings or requirements that your church has and then attempt to match the gifts that people display with such a list. However, we have to face the possibility that a small church may not be able to provide an outlet for every person. But if relationships in the church are strong, we do not need to worry about releasing or even helping a person to find an avenue for service outside of the local church. It will usually be the case that the benefits of a person's activity elsewhere will eventually bring benefit back to their own church. Even if it doesn't, it is surely better for our members to be released and serving than to remain with our church but never find their unique calling in Christ.

The ability of the local church to accommodate a very diverse range of gifts and ministries may well depend on its willingness to change the structures of the church. Most small churches work on the basis of a leadership structure which depends on appointments to certain positions and on the basis of finding people to perform certain tasks that need to be done. An alternative way of organising the church would be to say, 'we will only do those things that people are gifted for, so even if we have to experience a good deal of criticism, we will not run activities unless we have people who are clearly gifted and motivated to lead them'. For example, many churches feel obliged to offer a Sunday School programme whether or not they have people who are called to teach in such a situation. The result of using those who feel obligated to serve is that either the programme will be poor, or the people working in it will become unhappy with the church or both! In the first instance most churches who only operate programmes that people are gifted and called to, run far fewer activities. But in the long term, they see much more fruit.

Finally, do stay with the process. There are far too many small churches who begin a process of gift discovery only to give up halfway through, either because it is such a demanding process, or because other pressing matters arise, or even because no immediate fruit is obvious. Giving up halfway through can be very damaging for those whose hopes and expectations have been raised. It will make it difficult for your people to trust you on other matters. The members of your church are sufficiently valuable for you to succeed in this process no matter how long it might take.

Notes

1. Most notably 1 Corinthians 12;
2. Lesslie Newbigin, *The Gospel in a Pluralist Society*, (SPCK: 1990), p 231.
3. Arnold Bittlinger, *Gifts and Ministries*, (Hodder and Stoughton: 1974), p 20.
4. SIMA which stands for System for Identifying Motivated Abilities can be contacted at 62 Lime Walk, Headington, Oxford, OX3 7AE.
5. These five areas of activity are described in SIMA's publication, *Putting your Sima Portrait in Perspective*.
6. Bible Society has a spiritual gift discovery exercise in their church growth course. The School of World Mission based at Fuller, Pasedena, California publish a number of spiritual gift discovery exercises. Willow Creek Community Church of South Barrington, Chicago have devised a very sophisticated gift discovery programme. It is available in the U.S.A. through the Willow Creek Association and in the U.K through Scripture Press. See also Peter Wagner, *Your Spiritual Gifts Can Help Your Church Grow*, (Marc: 1986).

CHAPTER FIFTEEN

CALLED TO BE SMALL?

Occasionally, church leaders ask the question, 'Is there an ideal size for a church?' Somehow, a good number of people seem to have the idea that a church ought never to be larger than a certain predetermined size. The evidence of the New Testament suggests that churches were many sizes. The church in Jerusalem, immediately following the day of Pentecost was at least 3,000 strong and seemed to grow rapidly beyond that number.[1] It is also clear that there were many churches which met in homes which could be quite small groups. Paul met with a very small group of John's followers at Ephesus and after their conversion they went on to become a church of just twelve disciples.[2]

Some seem to take the view that once a church reaches a certain size, it ought to divide into at least two groups, as if a large church was somehow intrinsically undesirable. At the same time there is nothing especially virtuous about being a small church and we have to face the fact that some churches which are small now will not always be small. The Metropolitan Church, Whitewell in Belfast, has been a large church for some time. Attendance is close to 2,000 people on a Sunday, but for the first twelve years of its life was a small church. James McConnell, the minister of the Metropolitan Church has written a book which describes the history of his church.[3] The largest part of the book deals with the lessons that were learnt when the church was small. They were not called to be small for ever, but there was a time when that particular church was intended by God to be small and during that time the values and foundations of a much larger church were established.

Some churches are called to be small for a period of time. It is important to remember that the values of a small church do not have to be abandoned once a church begins to grow. The insight of some church growth thinkers that a larger church often has a structure which comprises of a large meeting, (a Celebration), several medium sized structures (a Congregation) and many very small groups (Cells),[4] can be helpful in allowing us to see how the values of a good small church can be maintained, even when a church which was small for a time begins to grow. There is nothing better about a church simply because it is either small, large or somewhere in between. They are simply different in their call.

Factors Which Serve to Keep a Church Small

Quite apart from the question of whether we are called to be small, there are some factors which have the effect of keeping a church small regardless of call. In assessing the nature of our call we need to be aware of the effect that these factors might have on our vision.

The size of our building

Although we all know that in theory it shouldn't work this way, it is astonishing how the size of a building has a tendency to both limit and define the vision of a church. This works in at least two ways. First, a small congregation that occupies a large building often feels defeated by the building. The sheer cost of repairing, maintaining and heating a building which is many times larger than the congregation requires, actually absorbs so much time and resource that the whole vision of the church becomes consumed simply by the task of keeping the building functioning. The result is that there is little energy left for a consideration of the mission of the church beyond that of simply keeping the doors open and the bills paid.

Secondly, a small church that also has a small building tends to feel that the mission has been accomplished once the building is comfortably full. Although in theory one could extend the building or even replace it, or move to more than one service in the same building, in practice, the degree of vision and energy that is required to overcome the inertia produced by the size of the building is sufficiently great that this rarely happens. It is much more likely, (though even then hardly common), for a small church whose life is overspilling the size of its building to think in terms of some kind of church plant.

This logistical problem has profound implications. Many small churches have buildings of a size, that only when they are completely full, could the congregation become large enough to think of supporting a full time minister, pay for the building costs and finance a well rounded programme of mission and outreach. In practice such congregations often go through a cycle of growth which takes place through the hard work and initiative of one individual. The enterprise of that one person will often take the congregation slightly beyond being a technically small congregation. But because the growth which they engender never takes the congregation beyond the size of the building, the congregation never becomes large enough for such life to be sustained. The consequence is that when that one individual either moves or ceases to be so focused on the church, growth settles back until the congregation gradually becomes once more a small congregation waiting for another highly gifted and committed person to emerge.

The history of the church

Some small congregations have a value system and internal culture which tends to keep the church small. The culture of the church will often relate to a time when many of those who are now members joined the church or even to when the church was first founded. In recent months I have visited two small churches where the majority of members joined the church within a few years of each other. In the case of one of those churches the majority of existing members joined during the early 1950's. That group of people were strong friends then, (indeed some were related through marriage), and have stayed friends ever since. They have brought up their children together and seen them marry and move away from home. It is very difficult for others who have joined the church in more recent times to break into the cultural norms which have been created through such a long-standing and personally meaningful circle of friendship. Significant growth in such a situation can only come through a radical change of culture within the church.

Other congregations have a history of conflict or division within the church which also ensures that the congregation will remain small. I remember visiting one congregation which was dominated by two families, the patriarchs of which had been arguing for at least half a century. Some commented that the reason both patriarchs were so old was that whoever died first lost the argument!

Leadership styles

We have already commented on the way in which Eddie Gibbs, in his book *I Believe in Church Growth* indicates how leadership styles need to change in relation to the size of a church.[5] One critical point at which change needs to occur is when a congregation reaches an upper limit of somewhere between 60 and 70 people. The appropriate leadership style for someone leading a congregation of less than this number is that of the leader of a work team. Such a leader is fully involved with the congregation as part of the team. So, if for example the church hall needs to be painted, the leader of the work team will be found with their sleeves rolled up participating fully in the task. Some leaders are particularly gifted at taking a very small group and building the team so that it reaches its full potential of 60 to 70 people, but are not able to make the necessary adjustments to allow the church to grow beyond this point. Should such a minister choose to stay as the leader, then the church will not grow beyond being a small church.

If any of the above factors apply then it is very likely that a small church will stay small. But this must not be confused with an actual call to be small. It may well be that a church is called to be small and also has some of these factors present, but the actual circumstances that comprise a call to be small are rather different. How can we recognise when a church is genuinely called to work out a mission which involves a specific call to remain as a fairly small group of believers?

When it is Good to Stay Small

Ministry to a specific area

The small church is the normal expression of church life in large parts of the country. In rural areas this reality reflects population density. It is not unusual for a rural parish to be no more than 300 people. In areas of low population density it is not possible to increase the number of people in the parish without making the distances that are travelled too great to allow a given community to be properly served. Given that some people in a population of 300 will want to travel some distance in order to attend a church of a particular denomination, and since there might also be a small Free church functioning in the community, it is hardly realistic to think that the Parish Church would ever have more than 50 regular participants in worship. Admittedly, special occasions such as Harvest and Christmas, might attract a higher percentage of people from the community, but many who attend on these occasions will never become part of the weekly worshipping community.

But the issue of ministry to a defined area also applies to many urban and suburban situations. Cities and towns are not single homogenous units. Every urban settlement is actually a complex fabric woven together by many smaller communities. The larger cities in our land expanded in the late nineteenth and early twentieth centuries by a process of absorbing many smaller communities. In the first decade of the twentieth century, Birmingham did not extend more than a mile in any direction from a fixed central point. Even today the residents of some communities think of themselves as belonging to a suburb before they consider themselves to be part of Birmingham. But the network of smaller communities is even more of a patchwork than just the older village communities which the city absorbed. It is fascinating to see how just a few streets in some areas have a very clear sense of community and see themselves as distinct, if not different, to the adjoining streets. These uncharted boundaries become very clear when such matters as Neighbourhood Watch schemes emerge.

Some smaller churches see themselves as ministering to areas sometimes no larger than a few streets around their buildings. Although they will rarely have drawn such boundaries on a map, there is an unspoken and often unconscious sense of attempting to meet the needs of a given area which may comprise no more than a few hundred homes. The boundaries become clear when observing the streets that are leafleted when a particular event is publicised, or by noting where the youngsters in an open youth group are primarily drawn from. In such a scenario there will even be those families who never attend the church but who regard themselves as in some sense belonging to such a community oriented church. The call of that church is to attempt to minister in some depth to that area.

Serving a special interest group

There are some groups in our society who are either resistant to the gospel or who do not live as large communities of people. The characteristics of these peoples are such that it will often require a specialised ministry to meet their needs. That ministry will sometimes result in the creation of a group which, whatever its official designation, is actually a church. The groups concerned might be as diverse as Pakistani converts from Islam, refugees from Sri Lanka, Christians from Hong Kong, Welsh speakers in Birmingham or a group of believers with hearing difficulties.

The particular needs of such groups of people sometimes means that it is either unrealistic or unhelpful to the people themselves to think of intergrating such believers into existing churches, however much we might like to work towards such a long term goal. Such specialist groups may officially be part of a larger mother church and may only be a separate congregation or ministry within another church, but the ties of fellowship and worship clearly mark them out as a small church with a specific call.

Care for broken people

Small churches often contain a higher percentage of needy people than larger churches do. Such a reality will be tiring, demanding and frustrating, but it may be more than just an obstacle to growth, it may constitute a call. When I worked in a small church in the inner city I remember one particular person who was very needy. She had difficulty reading, her health and hygiene were poor, she struggled to understand what benefits were available to her, and found it almost impossible to hold down a job. She had lived all of her life in the area close to where the church was located. Never in all that time had her family or neighbours extended much care to her. In part this was because those same neighbours and family members were very needy people also.

I watched with some joy over a number of years the way in which the love of ordinary members in our small church family changed the life of that one person. Church members helped her to improve her reading, they cleaned her flat and showed her how to keep it clean for herself. Some helped her with ideas for her diet and worked with her on some basic cooking lessons. The fellowship that she had in small house groups, the experiences on church outings, the joy in expressing herself in singing praises to God and in praying to him out loud and in public, these and many other expressions of church family life, acted to draw out the intrinsic beauty that she had as a child of God.

As I visit small churches I find them dealing on a daily basis with the irascible, the irritating, the unlovely and unloved, the unreasonable and the inadequate people of this world in a way that no-one else in our society would do. Here indeed is salt that flavours our world!

A frontier ministry

Some church situations are simply tough not because of the internal life of the church, but because the history of the neighbourhood in which the church is set makes the spread of the gospel very hard indeed. Often in such situations one is dealing with people who have not had any significant contact with the church, not just in their lifetime, but for many generations. Those who minister in such settings are engaged in the very primary work of mission.

Mission history around the world reveals that the early

frontier days of most missions were hard and the churches that were established were small. Eventually,in many places, the breakthrough came and large numbers of people did become Christians. But the work of breaking up the ground and sowing seeds was often undertaken by many small churches, some of whom never saw the immediate fruit of their labours. Such tough frontier ministry is the legitimate territory of the small church.

A resource group for the wider church

Occasionally I come across churches which are really a group of people who have been drawn together with the specific purpose of supporting a particular person, or group of people, who are offering a ministry to the whole church. It may be someone who is gifted in music or in drama, or in counselling or in a healing ministry. Often in such situations just one person is supported full time, whereas the others in the support group have secular employment and are involved as the providers of finance, prayer, encouragement and occasional travel when time permits. Some might argue that such a group of people are not a 'proper' church. But in terms of their internal life and their witness to others, whether friends or those in the community, it is hard to see why they should not be described as a church. The nature of their call may well ensure that they will always be small in numbers, even though their contribution to the whole church might be very significant.

Pioneering new forms of the church

What does it mean to be the church? There are those individuals who struggle with many of the expressions of the church that they see around them and yearn to explore new models. Some of those explorations might be fairly radical in style. Some are drawn together with like-minded individuals to experiment with community living or with informal churches that feel more like prayer groups than churches. Others might look more like discussion groups or even night clubs!

The heart of some of these groups may be to explore new forms of worship. They may be inspired by Taize, Iona, the late, late service in Glasgow or by their own creative drive.

These experimental groups may not be numerous, the group size may be small, and many may not last for long, but the lessons that they learn can be valuable to the wider church.

Bearing witness to particular insights

Some small churches come into being because they wish to bear witness to a particular insight or expression of church life or tradition that is simply not available in the other churches in a given area. This does not necessarily represent a sectarian spirit, since they may well see that insight as a gift to the whole church. They do not have to believe that everyone else should join their church in order to embrace such truth. Such expressions of the faith can be as diverse as a concern for believers baptism, to a conviction concerning the value of a Pentecostal experience, or even a zeal for a strongly reformed theology. In certain parts of the country it is almost inevitable that some groups which seek to give witness to a particular expression of the Christian faith will be small but the provision of such an option can be a very valuable contribution to the total Christian community.

Questions for the Small Church

The key question for the small church is not whether it can become large, (although as we have suggested, some may eventually become larger), so much as how it can know whether it is fulfilling its potential? Hopefully the preceding chapters will help every small church to make such an assessment of their life. Here we offer a few more questions for churches and the ministers of small churches to consider.

1. Are we making disciples?

The researcher Rosalie Osmond points out the difficulty that we sometimes have in distinguishing between Christian faith and a culture which has been significantly influenced by that faith. She quotes Lord Morris as saying 'The clergy are quite content to judge a man by his works and not by his faith, and especially a woman, if she comes along and cleans the brass and makes the cakes and sweeps the floor, then she's a *very* committed Christian. Nobody would *dare* ask her if she believed in the resurrection of the dead.'[6] There is a danger in the small church that we treat new members as joining our gang, rather than becoming fully informed followers of Jesus Christ. Yet whatever else we do, unless there is some evidence that disciples are being made we cannot claim to be a healthy church, regardless of our size.

2. Are we sure of our call?

Are we called to be a healthy small church, or are we only small because we have failed to fulfil some other call? Do we know what kind of mission that God has given us and do our members really feel called to engage in that mission?

3. Are we fulfilling our mission?

Is there some evidence that we are fulfilling the mission that we believe we are called to respond to? What is that evidence?

4. Does our mission need to change?

Is there some feeling in the church that the particular mission to which we have been called has now been fulfilled and that there needs to come an intentional reassessment of our mission?

5. Are there some clear obstacles in our way?

Some difficulties have to be lived with. Others are there not because they have to be endured, but because no one has so far had the courage to face them. Are there any such problems in our church, problems which have been present so long that they have become part of the landscape? Is this now the time to honestly face those problems? This can be hard because in the small church such problems are nearly always people problems!

6. If I am the minister or key leader, has my contribution gone as far as it can?

This question can be approached in at least two forms. First, a minister or key leader might discover that their training and gifts are actually better suited to leading a larger church. The idea that every minister should begin with a small church and then gradually trade in their smaller church for a better model until they arrive at a really large church is frankly ridiculous but widespread! Leading the small church requires particular skills and it is not a disgrace to conclude that you have a different gift or gifts.

Secondly, some leaders are simply very gifted at leading a small group of people and helping them grow to the point where their church can have a number of significant choices about their future size and mission. Having brought the church to the point where it is no longer a small group, it may well be necessary for that leader to move on and repeat the task with another small group of people. On occasion, a failure to end a ministry at this point may well mean that the person who has brought growth in the past may become the very obstacle that prevents the church from moving forward in the future. Moving a paid minister who has become an obstacle to growth may well be easier than removing a lay leader for whom the same is true, but it can still be very difficult and must be handled with sensitivity.

Small Can be Significant

When the small church feels very keenly its sense of call and mission and is well prepared to carry out that mission, then its impact can be out of all proportion to its actual size. In this sense, the small church is often larger than it appears to be. Small can be significant. The issue therefore is not a matter of size but of health. How then do we measure the health of a church?

In the Kingdom of God significance does not flow from size, but from faithfulness, and here the small church is often significant. I was struck recently by a passage in a book written by someone who has had a very fruitful ministry in South America and in Eastern Europe. Many have come to Christian faith and commitment through his work. In considering his family history he tells this story:

> Around the turn of the century a Danish immigrant, Carson Christiansen, settled a farm near Thief River Falls, Minnesota. He

was a Christian and once made an effort to influence a neighboring farmer couple, Peter and Anna, who were also Danish immigrants. Peter would have nothing to do with the subject, but Anna responded. She believed in Christ in 1922. Peter and Anna had four sons. In her concern for them, Anna sought out the local grocer, Art Hanson, whom she had heard was also a Christian. She persuaded him to employ one of her four sons, Arnold, a nineteen-year-old. This resulted in Arnold's believing in Christ. Arnold's fiancee, Eva, soon followed.

History does not remember either Carson Christiansen or Art Hanson. Both probably went to their graves thinking their lives had not amounted to much more than a lot of farming and grocery selling. They probably didn't even know they had been good seed. Arnold and Eva married and had six children. I'm one of those six. All six of us are indebted to those two unknown men, as the heritage we received has preserved our marriages and brought all our children, in turn, into God's family. As if that is not cause enough for celebration, the combined witness of our family has resulted in fruit that numbers into thousands and can be found all over the world[7]

The author of these words, Jim Peterson, comments, 'This same story has been replayed countless times over the past two thousand years. But it seldom makes the news, as it is virtually invisible'.[8] The faithful witness of many small churches may seem to be invisible when taken on a one to one basis, but that does not make that witness insignificant. The tapestry of Christian life and witness woven by the threads of many small churches has shaped the lives of many in our world and will continue to do so.

Faithfulness to the message of the Kingdom not only produces fruit in individual lives, it also creates communities of men and women who bear testimony to the values of the Kingdom. T S Eliot expresses this truth in the following lines.

> What life have you if you have not life together?
> There is no life that is not in community,
> And no community not lived in praise of God . . .
> And now you live dispersed on ribbon roads,
> And no man knows or cares who is his neighbour
> Unless his neighbour makes too much disturbance,

But all dash to and fro in motor cars,
Familiar with the roads and settled nowhere.

The journey of the small church does not result in dashing to and fro but in the formation of fellowship where men and women know each other and are known by each other. The healthy small church is anchored in the praise of God. That is cause for celebration!

Notes

1. Acts Chapter 2.
2. Acts Chapter 19: 1–7.
3. James McConnell, *Light on a Hill: the story of Whitewell Church*, (Marshall Pickering: 1987).
4. We have already referred to the principle of Cell, Congregation, and Celebration in Chapter 12 of this book. For reading see Chapter 12, footnote 4.
5. We have already discussed Eddie Gibb's work in Chapter 4 of this book.
6. Rosalie Osmond, *Changing Perspectives: Christian Culture and Morals in England Today*, (Darton, Longman and Todd: 1993), p 122f.
7. Jim Peterson, *Church Without Walls: Moving Beyond Traditional Boundaries*, (Navpress: Colorado Springs, 1992), p 60.
8. *Ibid*.

APPENDIX ONE

Lyle Schaller's example of how small churches are different:
[*The Small Church is Different*, pp 27–41]
 1. The small church is tough!
 2. The long-established Anglo church is usually built around a ministry of the laity.
 3. The small church is a volunteer organisation.
 4. The small church cares more for people than performance.
 5. The small church rewards generalists.
 6. The grapevine is an asset in the small church.
 7. The small church has a different system for the financial support of the congregation.
 8. The small church is intergenerational.
 9. The small church is relational.
 10. The small church uses an internal clock.
 11. The small church follows a different calendar.
 12. The small church has a place for everyone!
 13. Kinfolk ties are more important in the small church.
 14. Individuals, not committees, often do the work in small churches.
 15. The small church is often a participatory democracy.
 16. Social meetings dominate the agenda in the small church.
 17. The small church is easier to comprehend.
 18. A majority of small churches are subsidised.
 19. The small church tends to rely on an 'attraction' model in new-member recruitment.
 20. The piano often is the central musical instrument in the small church.

SELECT BIBLIOGRAPHY ON THE SMALL CHURCH

1. Books, papers and articles specifically on the small church

Activating Leadership in the Small Church, Steve Burt, (Judson Press, 1988). Part of the *Small Church in Action Series*, the author uses personal experience and humour as well as practical guidelines to illustrate the important work of motivating and enabling leadership, both pastoral and lay within the smaller church.

Developing Your Small Church's Potential, Carl S Dudley and Douglas Alan Walrath, (Judson Press, 1988). Another volume in the *Small Church in Action Series*. Dudley and Walrath offer valuable assistance in enabling small churches to face their culture, community, and the process of change within the congregation as well as ways the church can impact its surroundings.

Entering the World of the Small Church, Anthony G Pappas, (The Alban Institute, 1988). A real 'user's guide' to life within the small church and the kind of leadership which is required. His analysis of the small church as a folk society is especially helpful. Pappas also is editor of a newsheet which networks small churches in the USA.

Growing the Smaller Church, Mike Breen, (Marshall Pickering, 1992). As far as we know the only British book besides this one with "Small Church" in the title. However, it is not so much about the small church in general as it is the story of how one small church grew to become a much larger church.

Leading the Small Church, Doran McCarty, (Broadman Press, 1991). Published from the perspective of the Southern Baptists in the U.S.A., it nevertheless has some useful insights for pastors from other traditions as well.

Making the Small Church Effective, Carl S. Dudley, (Abingdon, Nashville, 1978). Highly recommended as a book which really understands the issues that face many small churches. Often called the 'Bible' of the small church.

Money, Motivation, and Mission in the Small Church, Anthony Pappas, (Judson Press, 1989). A further contribution to the *Small Church in Action Series*. Pappas tackles the thorny issues of money and mission with many valuable insights into how the small church thinks and feels on these important issues.

Preaching with the Small Congregation, Laurence A. Wagley, (Abingdon, 1989). The title conveys very well the particular concern of this book. Some helpful ideas.

Unique Dynamics of the Small Church, Carl S. Dudley, (Resources for People Who Care about Congregations, The Alban Institute, Washington, 1977). A resource paper that picks out one or two key issues in relation to the small church.

2. Books on Church Growth thinking and strategy

Close the Back Door, Alan F Harre, (Concordia, 1984). For those who are interested in how to stop people leaving the church, this is a good starter, but one should also consider *The Sheep that Got Away*, Michael Fanstone, (Monarch, 1993).

How Do Churches Grow?, Roy Pointer (MARC Europe, 1984). Probably the most helpful and concise guide on church growth yet published.

I Believe in Church Growth, Eddie Gibbs, (Hodder and Stoughton, revised 1990). A very comprehensive guide to church growth thinking.

Ready Steady Grow: Principles for the growth of the church in Britain, David Holloway, (Kingsway, 1989). A helpful and fairly brief summary of church growth thinking from someone well acquainted with the evangelical church in general and Anglican evangelicals in particular.

The Irrelevant Church, Robin Gamble, (Monarch, 1991). Gives a helpful account of the distance between the church and the working class together with some thoughts on what can be done about it.

3. Books on Leadership

Christian Leadership, David Spriggs, (Bible Society, 1993). More strongly pastoral and scripture related than many books which deal with the management issues of leadership.

Church on the Move, John Finney, (Daybreak, 1992). Finney's follow-up to *Understanding Leadership* which tackles the issues connected with assisting the church to face up to the challenges of mission in a secular context. He has particularly helpful comments on those outside the church as well as developing relevant strategies on evangelism.

Dynamic Leadership, Paul Beasley-Murray, (MARC, 1990). One of the most 'user-friendly' books on pastoral leadership, with many practical suggestions as to how to lead.

Followed or Pushed?, Eddie Gibbs, (MARC/BCGA, 1987). A very helpful volume on assisting each church leader to face up to the practical tasks and needed skills to lead churches of various styles, types and sizes.

How to Close Your Church In a Decade, David Cohen and Stephen Gaukroger, (Scripture Union, 1992). Both authors write their own suggestions and strategies in helping each church and its leadership face up to the challenge of the decade of evangelism before they become extinct.

Leading Your Church to Growth, Peter Wagner, (MARC, 1984). The application of church growth thinking to leadership issues.

Priorities, Planning and Paperwork, (MARC, 1992). A very practical volume on the needs of administration and forward thinking, along with discussions of useful time managment skills.

Understanding Leadership, John Finney, (Daybreak, 1989). A good introduction to the issues of leadership. Contains a good survey of other views.

Understanding Leadership, Tom Marshall, (Sovereign World, 1991). Brings many fresh and helpful insights to the subject of leadership. Highly recommended.

Vision Building, Peter Brierley, (Hodder & Stoughton, 1989). One of the better books on discovering, enhancing and implementing vision for leadership and churches. A most helpful section on working out the corporate vision, needed for all churches, regardless of size.

Your Spiritual Gifts Can Help Your Church Grow, Peter Wagner, (MARC, 1986). A helpful introduction to the subject of spiritual gifts.

4. Books on Religion and Society

A History of English Christianity 1920–1990, Adrian Hastings, (SCM 1991). Probably the best 20th century history of the church from the perspective of the major denominations.

British Social Attitudes: The Ninth Report, Social and Community Planning Research, Roger Jowell and others, (Dartmouth Publishing, 1992). A fascinating insight from a statistical point of view into British social attitudes in general with one excellent chapter on religious attitudes.

Church and Religion in Rural England, David, Watkins and Winter. (T & T Clark, 1991). A helpful insight into the particular issues that affect the rural church.

Faith in the City – A call for action by church and nation: The Report of the Archbishop of Canterbury's Commission on Urban Priority Areas, (Church House Publishing, 1985). The title is self explanatory.

Faith in the Countryside, (Churchman Publishing Ltd, 1990). The Archbishops' report on the state of the rural church with recommendations for the future.

Religion in Victorian Britain (Vol III Sources), James R Moore (Ed), (Manchester University Press, 1988). A useful collection of original sources on 19th century religion.

The Church in Town and Countryside Derek Baker (Ed), (Basil Blackwell, 1979). A collection of academic essays which give a picture of the church in various parts of Europe, North Africa and the Middle East at various times over the last 2,000 years.

The Gospel in a Pluralist Society, Lesslie Newbigin, (SPCK, 1990). Continues Newbigin's analysis of the impact of secularism on the mission of the church in the West.

British Church Growth Association

The British Church Growth Association was formed in September 1981 to help and encourage the church in Britain to move into growth in every dimension. The Association endeavours to offer practical help as well as encouraging and initiating church growth thinking and research.

Membership of the BCGA is open to both individuals and organisations interested in or involved in the theory or practice of church growth. Members receive the *Church Growth Digest* (the Association's journal) four times a year, information about activities through the Newsletters, special discounts and links with other researchers, teachers, practitioners, and consultants as well as help or advice on allied matters.

Further information is available from the Secretary, British Church Growth Association, 3a Newnham Street, Bedford, MK4 2JR, Tel: 0234 327905.